"The many events of life so easily pull us in all directions and make us lose our souls. But when we remain anchored in the heart of God, rooted in God's love, we have nothing to fear, not even death, and everything joyful and everything painful will give us a chance to proclaim the Kingdom of Jesus."

(from the book)

D0063434

HENRI J.M. NOUWEN

Our Second Birth

**CHRISTIAN REFLECTIONS ON
DEATH AND NEW LIFE**

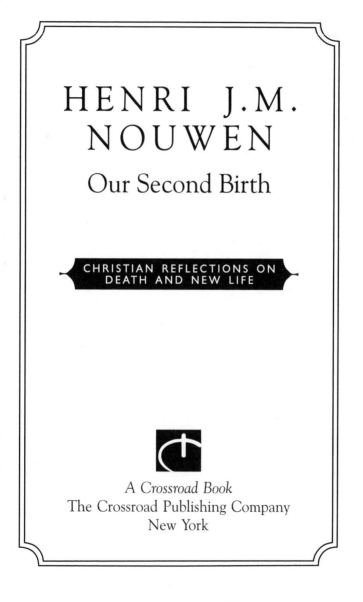

A Crossroad Book
The Crossroad Publishing Company
New York

5363

Material in this book excerpted from *Sabbatical Journey: A Diary of His Final Year*.

The Crossroad Publishing Company
16 Penn Plaza – 481 Eighth Avenue, Suite 1550
New York, NY 10001

Printed in the United States of America

The text is set in 11/15 Goudy Old Style.
The display font is Linoscript.

Library of Congress Cataloging-in-Publication Data

Nouwen, Henri J. M.
    Our second birth : Christian reflections on death and new life / Henri J.M. Nouwen.
        p.   cm.
    ISBN 0-8245-2365-2 (alk. paper)
    1. Death – Religious aspects – Catholic Church – Meditations.
2. Future life – Catholic Church – Meditations. 3. Nouwen, Henri J. M. I. Title.
BT825.N6855 2006
236.1 – dc22

                                                          2005031774

ISBN 13: 978-0-8245-2365-7

1 2 3 4 5 6 7 8 9 10   12 11 10 09 08 07 06

236.1
N8560

Contents

A Note from the Publisher

"I'm curious about Henri Nouwen — what's the first book I should read?" We hear this question constantly. We often suggest *Life of the Beloved* or *Return of the Prodigal Son* as good starting points. When serious fans ask us about a book that can take them more deeply into Nouwen's thought, we suggest *Sabbatical Journey*, a feast of intimate insights into what would become the final year of his life. We have long wanted to bring these two audiences together, abridging *Sabbatical Journey* in a way that could make its core insights into life, illness, death, and new birth accessible to the thousands of readers who, every year, turn to Nouwen for the first time. *Our Second Birth* is the culmination of this wish.

The root questions of life rarely change, and Nouwen's perceptive and rich writings on these questions are as compelling today as when he first penned the words some ten years ago. Whether seeing his father again, enjoying the hospitality of friends, or speaking with characteristic energy and charm to a small gathering, Nouwen was never clearer about the sacredness of life and the need to honor and embrace it fully. Nouwen's trust in Christ to bless this life and prepare us for the next life has never been more in evidence.

Whether you are a newcomer to Nouwen or a longtime reader, we hope you enjoy reading this book.

Our Second Birth

September 1995

This is the first day of my sabbatical. I am excited and anxious, hopeful and fearful, tired, and full of desire to do a thousand things. The coming year stretches out in front of me as a long, open field full of flowers and full of weeds. How will I cross that field? What will I have learned when I finally reach the other end?

During this weekend nine years ago, I arrived at Daybreak. I had just finished the journal in which I wrote down the many thoughts, emotions, passions, and feelings that led me to leave Harvard Divinity School and join "the Ark." It had taken me a year to make that transition. It was in fact my first sabbatical, during which my heart was gradually opened to a new life, a life with people with mental handicaps. *The Road to Daybreak* was the record of that sabbatical.

Now, exactly nine years later, I am sitting in my little apartment in the house of Hans and Margaret in Oakville, near Toronto. Hans and Margaret invited me to spend the first two weeks of my "empty year" with them, "just to relax." Hans said, "Just sleep, eat, and do what you want to do."

11

I feel strange! Very happy and very scared at the same time. I have always dreamt about a whole year without appointments, meetings, lectures, travels, letters, and phone calls, a year completely open to let something radically new happen. But can I do it? Can I let go of all the things that make me feel useful and significant? I realize that I am quite addicted to being busy and experience a bit of withdrawal anxiety. I have to nail myself to my chair and control these wild impulses to get up again and become busy with whatever draws my attention.

But underneath all these anxieties, there is an immense joy. Free at last! Free to think critically, to feel deeply, and to pray as never before. Free to write about the many experiences that I have stored up in my heart and mind during the last nine years. Free to deepen friendships and explore new ways of loving. Free most of all to fight with the Angel of God and ask for a new blessing. The past three months seemed like a steeplechase full of complex hurdles. I often thought, "How will I ever make it to September?" But now I am here. I have made it, and I rejoice.

One thing that helps me immensely is that the Daybreak community has sent me on this sabbatical. It is a mission! I am not allowed to feel guilty for taking a whole year off. To the contrary, I am supported to feel guilty when I am getting busy again. Although many of my Daybreak friends said, "We will miss you," they also said, "It is good for you and for us that you go." They affirm my vocation to be alone, read, write, and pray, and thus to live something new that can bear fruit not only in my own life but also in the life of our community. It is such a support for me that I can live my time away not only as a way of doing my will but also as a way of doing the will of the community. I can even think of it as an act of obedience!

Last night, Hans and his daughter Maja came to Daybreak to participate in the Friday night Eucharist and to pick me up. As we drove to Oakville, Hans said, "I came to be sure that you had no excuse to stay another day."

Right now I have no excuses for anything but to embark on a new journey and to trust that all will be well. It is clear to me that I have to keep a journal again, just as I did during the year before coming to Daybreak. I have promised myself not to let a day pass without writing down, as honestly and directly as possible, what is happening within and around me. It won't be easy, since I don't know the field I am entering. But I am ready to take a few risks.

I am starting this year with the prayer of Charles de Foucauld, the prayer I say every day with much trepidation:

> Father, I abandon myself into your hands.
> Do with me whatever you will.
> Whatever you may do, I thank you.
> I am ready for all, I accept all.
> Let only your will be done in me,
> and in all your creatures.

13

Into your hands I commend my spirit.
I offer it to you with all the love that is in my heart.
For I love you, Lord, and so want to give myself,
to surrender myself into your hands,
without reserve and with boundless confidence,
for you are my Father.

Amen.

Sunday, September 3

My unconscious certainly has not gone on sabbatical yet! Last night was full of the wildest and most chaotic dreams. Dreams about not making it on time for a meeting, not being able to keep up with all my obligations, and not finishing anything that I was supposed to finish. My dreams were full of people who were angry with me for not doing what they asked me to do, and full of letters and faxes that urgently needed responses. Every time I woke up between my dreams and found myself in the quiet, peaceful, guest room of my friends, without any plans for today, I laughed. The only thing I could say was that simple prayer, "Lord Jesus Christ, have mercy on me."

Prayer is the bridge between my unconscious and conscious life. Prayer connects my mind with my heart, my will with my passions, my brain with my belly. Prayer is the way to let the life-giving Spirit of God penetrate all the corners of my being. Prayer is the divine instrument of my wholeness, unity, and inner peace.

14

So what about my life of prayer? Do I like to pray? Do I want to pray? Do I spend time praying? Frankly, the answer is no to all three questions. After sixty-three years of life and thirty-eight years of priesthood, my prayer seems as dead as a rock. I remember fondly my teenage years, when I could hardly stay away from the church. For hours I would stay on my knees filled with a deep sense of Jesus' presence. I couldn't believe that not everyone wanted to pray. Prayer was so intimate and so satisfying. It was during these prayer-filled years that my vocation to the priesthood was shaped. During the years that followed I have paid much attention to prayer, reading about it, writing about it, visiting monasteries and houses of prayer, and guiding many people on their spiritual journeys. By now I should be full of spiritual fire, consumed by prayer. Many people think I am and speak to me as if prayer is my greatest gift and deepest desire.

The truth is that I do not feel much, if anything, when I pray. There are no warm emotions, bodily sensations, or mental visions. None of my five senses is being touched — no special smells, no special sounds, no special sights, no special tastes, and no special movements. Whereas for a long time the Spirit acted so clearly through my flesh, now I feel nothing. I have lived with the expectation that prayer would become easier as I grow older and closer to death. But the opposite seems to be happening. The words *darkness* and *dryness* seem to best describe my prayer today.

Maybe part of this darkness and dryness is the result of my overactivity. As I grow older I become busier and spend less and less time in prayer. But I probably should not blame myself in that way. The real questions are, "What are the darkness and the dryness about? What do they call me to?" Responding to these questions might well be the main task of my sabbatical. I know that Jesus, at the end of his life, felt abandoned by God. "My God, my God," he cried out on the cross, "why have you forsaken me?" (Mt 27:46). His body had been destroyed by his torturers, his mind was no longer able to grasp the meaning of his existence, and his soul was void of any consolation. Still, it was from his broken heart that water and blood, signs of new life, came out.

Are the darkness and dryness of my prayer signs of God's absence, or are they signs of a presence deeper and wider than my senses can contain? Is the death of my prayer the end of my intimacy with God or the beginning of a new communion, beyond words, emotions, and bodily sensations?

As I sit down for half an hour to be in the presence of God and to pray, not much is happening to talk about to my friends. Still, maybe this time is a way of dying with Jesus.

The year ahead of me must be a year of prayer, even though I say that my prayer is as dead as a rock. My prayer surely is, but not necessarily the Spirit's prayer in me. Maybe the time has come to let go of *my* prayer, *my* effort to be close to God, *my* way of being in communion with the Divine, and to allow the Spirit of God to blow freely in me. Paul writes, "What you received was not the spirit of slavery to bring you back into fear; you received the spirit of adoption, enabling us to cry out, 'Abba, Father!' The living Spirit joins with our spirit to bear witness that we are children of God" (Rom 8:14–16).

My wild, unruly dreams will probably keep reminding me of the great spiritual work ahead of me. But I trust that it is not just I who have to do the work. The Spirit of God joins my spirit and will guide me as I move into this blessed time.

Monday, September 4

Last night I drove to downtown Toronto to have dinner with Nathan and Sue. Nathan is the director of Daybreak, and Sue its pastor, replacing me during my sabbatical. We came together just to affirm the friendship between us that has grown during the past nine years. Nathan and I came to Daybreak on the same day, and Sue, who has lived at Daybreak during most of its twenty-five years of existence, was one of the main voices calling me to Canada to become member and pastor of the community. The three of us not only live in the same community and work together in many ways but also have become close friends. Last night was a night to celebrate that friendship.

As I reflect on the year ahead, I realize that friendship will be as important a concern as prayer. Maybe even more important. My need for friendship is great, greater than seems "normal." When I think about the pains and joys of my life, they have little to do with success, money, career, country, or church, but everything to do with friendships. My friendship with Nathan and Sue proves that clearly. The moments of ecstasy and agony connected with both of them mark my nine years at Daybreak.

I have felt rejected as well as supported, abandoned as well as embraced, hated as well as loved. All through it I have come to discover that friendship is a real discipline. Nothing can be taken for granted, nothing happens automatically, nothing comes without concentrated effort. Friendship requires trust, patience, attentiveness, courage, repentance, forgiveness, celebration, and most of all faithfulness. It is amazing for me to realize how often I thought that it was all over, that both Nathan and Sue had betrayed me or dropped me, and how easily feelings of jealousy, resentment, anger, and depression came over me. It is even more amazing to see that we are still friends, yes, the best of friends. But it certainly has been hard work for all three of us.

My question as I leave Daybreak for a year is, "How can I live my friendships during this time?" Am I going to feel that out of sight means out of mind and give in to despair? Or can I move to a new inner place where I can trust that both presence and absence can deepen the bond of friendship? Most likely I will experience both ends of the spectrum of human relationship. I had better be prepared for it. But whatever I will "feel," it is important that I keep making inner choices of faithfulness.

In this respect, my struggle with prayer is not so different from my struggle with friendship. Both prayer and friendship need purification. They need to become less dependent on fleeting emotions and more rooted in lasting commitments. As I write this, it sounds very wise! But I know already that my body and soul might need an immense amount of discipline to catch up with this wisdom. . . .

Wednesday, September 6

From the bay windows of Hans and Margaret's house I have a splendid view of Lake Ontario. My eyes are continually drawn to the mysterious line where water and sky touch each other. It is blue touching gray, or gray touching blue, or blue touching blue, or gray touching gray. Endless shades of blue and endless shades of gray. It is like an abstract painting in which everything is reduced to one line, but a line that connects heaven and earth, soul and body, life and death.

Just focusing on that line is meditating. It quiets my heart and mind and brings me a sense of belonging that transcends the limitations of my daily existence. Most often the water and sky are empty, but once in a while a sailboat or a plane passes by in the distance, neither of them ever crossing the line. Crossing the line means death. . . .

Thursday, September 7

Last night I called Cardinal Joseph Bernardin, the archbishop of Chicago, to ask him about his health. He said, "Henri, I'm so glad to hear from you. Yesterday I went back to work, half days. I am doing really well." His voice was strong and energetic. I said, "Ever since I visited you in July I've been thinking of you a lot and praying for you, and I'm so glad that you feel so well and are ready to go to work again." Then he said, "I can't tell you, Henri, how much it meant to me that you came to see me, prayed with me, and gave me some of your books. Thanks again. This truly is a time of special graces for me."

I vividly remember my visit to the cardinal in July. At that time I was at the National Catholic HIV/AIDS Ministries Conference in Chicago. The newspapers had widely reported that Cardinal Bernardin was suffering from pancreatic cancer and had undergone intensive surgery and follow-up radiation treatments. Soon after I arrived in Chicago, my priest friend Bob called to say that the cardinal would like me to visit him.

I spent half an hour talking and praying with him. I was deeply moved by our conversation. He told me about Steven, who had falsely accused him of sexual abuse and had later withdrawn his accusation. It had been major news and had caused great suffering for the cardinal. After it was all over he decided to visit Steven in Philadelphia and offer him his forgiveness, pray with him, and celebrate the Eucharist. Steven, who lives with AIDS and had very hostile feelings toward the church, was deeply touched by this gesture of reconciliation. For Joseph Bernardin as well as for Steven this had been a most important moment of life, a moment of true healing.

"Now both Steven and I are severely ill, Steven with AIDS and I with cancer," the cardinal said. "We both have to prepare ourselves for death. Steven calls me nearly once a month to ask me how I am doing. That means a lot to me. We are now able to support each other."

As the cardinal was telling me this, I started to feel very close to him. He really is a brother to me, a fellow human being, struggling as I do. I found myself calling him Joseph and dropping the words "Cardinal" and "Your Eminence."

"This is a very graced time," Joseph said. "As I go to the hospital for treatment, I do not want to go through the side door directly to the doctor's office. No, I want to visit the other patients who have cancer and are afraid to die, and I want to be with them as a brother and friend who can offer some consolation and comfort. I have a whole new ministry since I became ill, and I am deeply grateful for that."

We spoke about death. My mother had died after surgery for pancreatic cancer, so I knew how dangerous Joseph's illness was. Although he was very optimistic and expected to survive and be able to return to his work, he was not afraid to talk about his death. As I sat with him I became deeply convinced that his illness and possible death might be the greatest gift he has to offer to the church today. So many people are dying of AIDS and cancer, so many people are dying through starvation, war, and violence. Could Joseph's illness and death become a true compassionate ministry to all these people? Could he live it as Jesus did, for others? I was so grateful that he didn't go through the back door to the hospital but through the front door, visiting the patients. I was so grateful that Steven, living with AIDS, is there to encourage him. I am so grateful that he is willing to drink the cup of sorrow and to trust that this is his finest hour.

Obviously I hope that Joseph will completely recover from his cancer, and I am very glad to know that he has returned to his work. In my view Cardinal Joseph Bernardin is one of the most significant leaders in the Catholic Church today, and I know how much his people in Chicago hope that he will be able to continue his leadership.

Still, Joseph will die someday. His illness has confronted him with the closeness of death. I pray that what he has lived this year with Steven and his own cancer will make the time ahead of him, whether short or long, the most compassionate time of his life, a time that can bear fruit far beyond the boundary of his death.

Friday, September 8

Last night the Toronto International Film Festival started. It will last until September 16 and bring hundreds of new films from different countries and cultures to the city. Hans bought the richly illustrated catalog in which all the films are described and gave it to me to "study."

Going through the pages of the catalog, it strikes me that this is a contemporary storybook. Each film tells a story about how people live, suffer, and die. Most stories are about human relationships, gentle and caring, violent and abusive. All of them offer glimpses of what our world is like today, in Africa, Asia, Latin America, Australia, and North America.

Although the catalog is subtitled *Nourishment for a Modern Age*, much of the food tastes quite bitter. Ours is certainly an age of immense confusion, radical upheavals, and emotional and moral bewilderment. But in the midst of it all there is heroism, kindness, sacrifice, and a deep yearning for belonging. I can hardly think of a better way to learn about the human aspirations at the end of the twentieth century than through this festival. The stories that it tells are the stories of men, women, and children of our day and age. One might object by saying that most of these stories are abnormal or exceptional, but it does not take much to realize that they are touching the most sensitive nerves of our society.

It is very hard, if not impossible, to get tickets for any of these films at this late date. They were sold out long before the beginning of the festival. People want to see and hear stories and experience their own stories in the context of larger, maybe more dramatic, more explicit, or more intense ones. I have written many essays, reflections, and meditations during the last twenty-five years. But I have seldom written a good story. Why not? Maybe my moralistic nature made me focus more on the uplifting message that I felt compelled to proclaim than on the often ambiguous realities of daily life, from where any uplifting message has to emerge spontaneously. Maybe I

23

have been afraid to touch the wet soil from which new life comes forth and anxious about the outcome of an open-ended story. Maybe. But I am sure that we all want to hear stories, from the moment we are born to the moment we die. Stories connect our little lives with the world around us and help us discover who we are. The Bible is a storybook, and the Gospels are four stories about the birth, death, and resurrection of Jesus, who himself was one of the greatest storytellers.

As I begin this sabbatical year I realize that as a priest I must become a storyteller. I have many stories to tell. The first question is, "How can I tell them well?" It is not easy to tell a story, certainly not when you have an inclination to run quickly toward a happy ending. The second question is, "How can I find the courage to write stories that don't fit a prefabricated frame?"

Whatever is ahead of me, the Toronto International Film Festival is a clarion call to write stories and not be afraid.

Sunday, September 10

Each evening before dinner I celebrate the Eucharist in the dining room with Hans and Margaret and their guests.

I am always grateful for the opportunity to bring friends together for prayer before we share a meal. Listening to the readings from the Bible, reflecting on their significance for our lives today, praying for the many people of whose needs we are aware, and receiving the Body and Blood of Jesus unite us in a way that no good conversation or good meal can accomplish. The Eucharist indeed makes us church — *ecclesia* — which means people called away from slavery to freedom. Yes, we are family, we are friends, we are business associates. But more than that we are people of God journeying together to our home, the place where Jesus went to prepare a place for us.

There is much to enjoy in life, but unless it can be enjoyed as a foretaste of what we will see and hear in the house of God, our mortality will easily make all pleasure vain, transitory, and even empty.

The second reading today (Phlm 10, 12–17) is a part of the remarkable letter that Paul wrote to Philemon to plead for Onesimus, a runaway slave whom Paul had converted to Christ while in prison.

This letter is a masterpiece. There is affection for Philemon and his slave Onesimus, there is persuasive arguing asking Philemon to take his fugitive slave back not as a slave but as a brother. There is even some subtle cunning, suggesting that Philemon owes Paul a favor. Paul is "prudent as a snake and gentle as a dove." His deep love for Onesimus is obvious. Indeed he would have liked Onesimus to remain where he was. But Philemon, most likely a landowner in Colossae and a convert of Paul, is a powerful man, and Paul doesn't want to alienate him. So he sends Onesimus back to his owner, but not without loading some hot coals on his head. He writes, "If he has wronged you in any way, or owes you anything, charge that to my account. I, Paul, am writing this with my own hand: I will repay it" (Phlm 18–19).

But then he adds in a nearly mischievous way, showing that he does not expect to pay anything, "I say nothing about your owing me even your own self." In Paul's opinion, Philemon's conversion is worth a lot more than whatever Onesimus might owe him, and if he takes his conversion — and his personal relationship with Paul — seriously, he had better treat Onesimus in the way Paul wants him to!

To be in the world without being of the world, to use the tactics of the world in the service of the Kingdom, to respond to people with wealth in a fearless way, convinced that you have more to offer than to receive, to plead for the poor in ways that the rich can understand, to carry the Gospel in one hand, a stick in the other . . . all of that is part of Paul's militant servanthood. It is also part of our common journey home.

We might think about ourselves as converted slaves who continue to live in this world and ask our many "bosses" to treat us as brothers and sisters. Not every Philemon in our lives will respond favorably to our request. It might not hurt to have with us a letter such as Paul wrote. Sometimes we might even have to write such a letter to our converted friends!

Monday, September 11

Why am I so tired? Although I have all the time I want to sleep, I wake up with an immense feeling of fatigue and get up only because I want to do some work. But I feel extremely frustrated. I want to write, read, and respond to some people's requests, but everything requires an immense effort, and after a few hours of work I collapse in utter exhaustion, often falling into a deep sleep. I expected that I would be tired after the intense and busy summer, but now, after ten quiet days, it feels that the more I rest the more tired I become. There seems no end to it.

Fatigue is a strange thing. I can push it away for a long time. I can go on automatic, especially when there are many routine things to do. But when finally the space and time are there to do something new and creative, all the repressed fatigue comes back like a flood and paralyzes me.

I am quite possessive about my time. I want to use it well and realize some of my long-cherished plans. I can't tolerate wasting time, even though I want to write about wasting time with God, with friends, or with the poor! There are so many contradictions within me.

Hans keeps laughing at me. "You are here to relax, to turn off your busyness, but you are living your vacation as a big job!" He is right, but the distance between insight and practice is huge.

The real question for me is how to live my fatigue as an experience that can deepen my soul. How can I live it patiently and fully experience its pains and aches?

But I am not the only one who is tired. When I walk in downtown Toronto, I can see fatigue on the faces of the men and women moving quickly from one place to another. They look preoccupied, thinking about family, work, and the many things they have to do before the night falls. And when I look at the faces that appear on the television newscasts from Bosnia, Rwanda, and many other war-torn places, it feels like all of humanity is tired, more than tired, exhausted.

Somewhere I have to connect my little fatigue with the great fatigue of the human race. We are a tired race, carrying a burden that weighs us down. Jesus says, "Come to me, you who are tired and feel the burden of life. Take on my burden — which is the burden of the whole world — and you will discover that it is a light burden." It moves me deeply that Jesus says not "I will take your burden away" but "Take on God's burden."

So what is God's burden? Am I tired simply because I want to do my thing and can't get it done, or am I tired because I am carrying something larger than myself, something given to me to alleviate the burdens of others?

Thursday, September 14

This is the end of my time here. I will return to Daybreak for the weekend and then drive to Boston, where I plan to stay until Christmas.

The weekend at Daybreak will be important for me. Six friends will visit the community from Friday until Sunday. The community decided that this would also be a good occasion to "officially" send me on my sabbatical. That will happen during the Eucharist tomorrow evening.

Utica, New York, Sunday, September 17

At noon Nathan picked me up to drive with me to Boston, where I will be with my friend Robert Jonas and his family until Christmas. I had worried about doing the twelve-hour drive from Toronto to Boston alone, and I am deeply grateful that Nathan was willing to drive me there and take a plane back to Toronto so that I could have my car in Boston. We made it as far as Utica, New York.

Watertown, Massachusetts Monday, September 18

A beautiful, sunny day. We left Utica at 9:00 a.m. and arrived at Jonas and Margaret's home at 2:00 p.m. The long drive gave us the opportunity to talk about many things, including my community send-off and the visit of our guests over the weekend. We also spoke about illness and death. Nathan said, "Tell me what you want if you should get in a serious accident or become terminally ill." It was good to talk about this, since I had just made a "living will" and given Nathan the authority to act in my name. I told him about my gratitude for the life I have lived so far and my desire not to be kept alive artificially, or to have any organ transplant or extraordinary surgery. I said, "I do not feel any desire to die soon, but in case of an accident or serious illness I am ready to die, and I want you to feel empowered to discontinue life support when there is no real hope of recovery." "And when you die? What do you want to happen?" Nathan asked.

I thought a little and said, "I do not want to control my own funeral or burial. That's a worry I do not need! But if you want to hear my preference, then I can say this: Keep me away from a funeral home, make a simple wooden coffin in our woodery, let people say good-bye in the Dayspring chapel, and bury me in a plot at Elgin Mills Cemetery, where other members of Daybreak can also be buried. And . . . keep it very simple, very prayerful, and very joyful."

We also talked a little about my unpublished writing: letters, notebooks, and so on. I told Nathan that I had given Sue the authority to use her own judgment about what should be published. The idea of people posthumously exploring the details of my personal life frightens me, but I am reassured by the knowledge of having friends who know me intimately and will guard me not only in life but also in memory.

Jonas, Margaret, and their five-year-old son, Samuel, live in a beautiful home in Watertown, outside of Boston. Margaret's mother, Sarah, has a lovely apartment on the third floor and has offered it to me for the next three months while she is on retreat at the Insight Meditation Center in Barre, Massachusetts. I am very excited about this arrangement. There is solitude and community, distance from Toronto but closeness too, a very quiet home but near a city with all the bookstores and libraries anyone could want, and, most of all, time to write and time to be with very good friends.

Jonas, Margaret, and Sam welcomed us warmly. Sarah joined us for dinner. We talked about Margaret's and Jonas's plans for the fall, Sarah's upcoming retreat, Sam's first piano lesson, and Nathan's and my own dreams for the future. . . .

It feels very good to be here, and I can hardly believe that I finally have reached the place I have dreamt about for so long.

Tuesday, September 19

At 6:30 a.m. Jonas and I drove Nathan to Logan Airport. I give thanks to God for the gift of his friendship.

Jonas and I met during the early eighties while I was teaching at Harvard Divinity School. He came to a lecture I gave at St. Paul's Church in Cambridge and asked whether I could offer him some spiritual guidance. Soon it became clear that I could use his guidance as much as he could use mine, and a friendship started to grow. Today I marvel at the many ways our lives became connected. When I left Harvard to go to Europe for a year, Jonas came to see me twice, and after I joined L'Arche Daybreak in Toronto, he also came to visit. He became a friend of the community and developed warm relationships with Nathan, Sue, Carl, and many other Daybreak members. After Jonas married Margaret in 1986, I became a friend of the new family. In the years that followed Margaret and Jonas strengthened and deepened their professional as well as personal lives. Jonas, a psychotherapist, acquired a master of theological studies degree, while Margaret was ordained to the Episcopal priesthood by Bishop Barbara Harris. On December 6, 1989, their son, Samuel, was born, and on July 29, 1992, their daughter, Rebecca, was born. She lived only a few hours, and then died in Jonas's arms.

One of the special joys of the last ten years has been occasionally to give retreats and workshops with Jonas, who is a wonderful musician. The amelodic music he plays on the shakuhachi, a Japanese bamboo flute, allows people to experience God's spirit in ways that words cannot express. Over the years we have complemented each other quite well and enjoyed letting our friendship become fruitful in the lives of others.

While at Harvard, before I even knew Jonas or Margaret, I met Sarah. I remember how impressed I was by her peaceful and gentle spirit. I am filled with awe that I will now be living with Jonas, Margaret, and Sam, and using Sarah's apartment as my hermitage.

Wednesday, September 20

This morning, while Margaret took Sam to kindergarten, Jonas and I celebrated the Eucharist in the Empty Bell, a small, very beautiful meditation center behind Jonas and Margaret's house. Originally it was a large two-car garage. The Empty Bell is the realization of Jonas's longtime dream to integrate his psychotherapeutic formation with his skills as a spiritual guide, and to create a place where people from different religious traditions can meet and pray.

What better place could there be for me to live my sabbatical? A place where psychology and spirituality meet, a place of prayer and contemplation, a place of family life and interreligious dialogue, a place of solitude and a place of friendship, a place for children and adults. This is not a big center or gathering place. It is very simple, small, and intimate.

The Empty Bell has a little vestibule where people can take off their shoes and prepare themselves to go to the prayer room on the second floor. The prayer room is an empty space — not barren, cold, or forbidding but quiet, spacious, and inviting. The ceiling is white with wooden crossbeams and indirect lights. On the wooden floor, cushions are placed in a circle. A large, saucer-shaped bell, which gives a beautiful, resonant sound when struck at the rim, closes the circle. On the windowsills different Oriental flutes are placed.

For Jonas the Empty Bell is a place where body, mind, and spirit can find healing and integration. I am deeply convinced that the Empty Bell will also become a place to renew and strengthen my own spiritual life.

Thursday, September 21

At 8:30 this morning I joined a group of nine people who come every other Thursday morning to the Empty Bell for a time of meditation and reflection. After playing the shaku-hachi for a few minutes to help us quiet down, Jonas gave a short instruction about "staying with your breathing." Then we meditated for twenty minutes and listened to the Gospel story in which Jesus calls Matthew, the tax collector, with the words "Follow me." This story became the focus of a time in which each one of us sitting in the circle offered some personal reflections. Finally we all prayed.

It was a simple but very beautiful time. Although I knew only two people in the circle, there was a spiritual intimacy among us that could only be understood as a sign of God's presence.

In the afternoon, Sarah showed me her apartment and told me how to use it during her absence. A few hours later she left on her three-month retreat. Before she stepped into her car, Margaret, Sam, Sarah, and I embraced while I prayed. I asked God that Sarah's time in solitude would bear fruit not only in her own heart but in the hearts of many people.

Sarah looked gratefully at me and said, "Yes, my time away is a time for others." Then she drove off.

I feel very connected with Sarah. I am sure that her soli-tude at the Insight Meditation Center and my solitude in her apartment will greet each other and support each other. I think about it as a Buddhist-Christian dialogue of the heart.

Tonight I will move from my room into Sarah's apartment on the third floor of Jonas and Margaret's home. It is another beginning!

Saturday, September 23

It's a little game, but it works. I bought a little notebook with a hard cover portraying the Angel from the Pérussis Altarpiece at the Metropolitan Museum of Art. The book is called "Museum Notes" and contains 160 blank pages of acid-free paper.

Tom and John of HarperSanFrancisco have asked me to make a yearbook with a thought a day. I wondered how I could do that considering the fact that a year has 365 days. I don't think I have that many new thoughts, or, for that matter, that many old ones!

But my Museum Notes book helps me a lot. I write a few thoughts each day and have decided not to use more than one page for each thought and to leave the opposite page free for corrections.

It is indeed becoming a game. I sit at my desk and say to myself, "Do you have a thought for your Angel?" Usually something emerges in my mind when I bring my ballpoint to the paper. Today I even surprised myself with eight thoughts. When I have filled my book with eighty thoughts, I will send it to Toronto and ask my secretary, Kathy, to put them on the computer. Then I can read them all and see how often I repeated myself. Right now I am not looking backward! It does worry me a bit that I have to fill nearly five of these notebooks before Tom and John are going to be content. However, it is only September; there are many days to write in my Angel book.

Sunday, September 24

Last night I saw the film *Apollo 13* for the second time at a small theater in Watertown with Jonas and Margaret. When we came home, Margaret showed me the photo book *The Home Planet*, conceived and edited by Kevin W. Kelley for the Association of Space Explorers.

Looking at the magnificent photographs of planet Earth taken from outer space, and reading the comments of the astronauts and cosmonauts, I had a sense of being introduced to a new mysticism. The observations made from outer space seem very similar to those made from inner space. They both reveal the precariousness of life, the unity of the human family, the responsibility of the "seer," the power of love, and the mystery of God. James Irwin, who flew on *Apollo 15* in July 1971, writes:

> The Earth reminded us of a Christmas tree ornament hanging in the blackness of space. As we got farther and farther away it diminished in size. Finally it shrank to the size of a marble, the most beautiful marble you can imagine. That beautiful, warm, living object looked so fragile, so delicate, that if you touched it with a finger it would crumble and fall apart. Seeing this has to change a man, has to make a man appreciate the creation of God and the love of God.

All the astronauts and cosmonauts were overwhelmed by the unspeakable beauty of their own home, the planet Earth, and in some way or another raised the question "How can we care better for our own home?" Seeing your home planet as a precious little gem that needs care and protection is a deeply mystical experience that can only be captured by words such as *grace* and *responsibility*. Russell Schweickart, who flew on *Apollo 9* in 1969, writes:

> You think about what you are experiencing and why. Do you deserve this, this fantastic experience? Have you earned this in some way? Are you separated out to be touched by God, to have some special experience that others cannot have? And you know that the answer to that is no. There's nothing you've done to deserve this, to earn this; it's not a special thing for you. You know very well at that moment, and it comes through to you so powerfully, that you're the sensing element for man. You look down and see the surface of that globe that you've lived on all this time, and you know all those people down there, and they are like you, they are you, and somehow you represent them. You're up here as the sensing element, that point out on the end, and that's a humbling feeling. It's a feeling that says you have a responsibility. It's not for yourself. The eye that doesn't see doesn't do justice to the body. That's why it's there; that's why you are out there. And somehow you recognize that you are a piece of this total life. And you're out there on that forefront and you have to bring it back

somehow. And that becomes a rather special responsibility, and it tells you something about your relationship with this thing we call life. So that's a change. That's something new. And when you come back there's a difference in that world now. There's a difference in that relationship between you and that planet and you and all those other forms of life on that planet, because you've had that kind of experience. It's a difference and it's so precious.

It is a mystic, a seer, who speaks here. Isaiah could have said this or Joan of Arc or John of the Cross. What they saw evoked deep humility and great responsibility. They experienced their vision as a grace and as a call, as a gift not just for themselves but for all of humanity. What is experienced as most intimate is lived out as most universal. The human heart unites with the heart of the universe, and this unity becomes the source of a new mission.

The "seers" are like holy men who have a special radiance because of what they have seen. Robert Cenker, who flew on *Columbia 7* in January 1986, writes:

Of all the people I've spoken to about the experience of space, only those closest to me can begin to understand. My wife knows what I mean by the tone of my voice. My children know what I mean by the look in my eye. My parents know what I mean because they watched me grow up with it. Unless you actually go and experience it yourself you will never really know.

That's the loneliness of the mystic. Having seen and experienced what cannot be expressed in words and still must be communicated. The astronauts and cosmonauts gave words to my own experience of priesthood. It is a grace, it allows me to see a vision, and it is a call to let others know what I have seen; it is a long loneliness and an inexpressible joy.

Monday, September 25

...In the Gospel today, Jesus says, "For there is nothing hidden, except to be disclosed; nor is anything secret, except to come to light" (Mk 4:22). These words encourage me to live my "hidden and secret life" well. I have to trust that the more faithful I am to my solitude, the more fruitful it will be in my community. I realize now how important it is to live this time with a pure heart. My most intimate thoughts and feelings will somehow, somewhere come to light. I pray that, placed in the light, they will delight those who see them.

Saturday, September 30

Jonas invited me to join his Buddhist-Christian dialogue group for lunch. There was a Zen Buddhist monk, a Tibetan Buddhist nun, a Catholic priest, a Catholic nun, a Catholic married woman, Jonas, and myself. The discussion was animated and cordial.

What struck me most were the different wavelengths on which Catholics and Buddhists think. It seems that Catholics, independent of any particular subject, are mostly concerned about authority and doctrine. Somehow there is an "in or out" kind of thinking, even when the boundaries might be quite movable. "What is the truth and who has it?" is a question not explicitly stated but seeming always to be there unconsciously. The Catholic Church has a very explicit set of teachings and a very visible hierarchy among those who announce, protect, and defend these teachings.

Buddhists don't think that way. For them, explicit doctrines prevent inner freedom, and true authority is rooted in the degree to which one has acquired that inner freedom. Buddhists don't divide their world between those who are "in" and those who are "out." Their spiritual goal is to find the place of limitless compassion, where all is nothing and nothing is all.

Is there a place for a Buddhist-Christian dialogue when the word itself is a questionable instrument of communication? I think it is of great importance that Buddhists and Christians meet. There is so much they have to give to each other. But maybe instead of *dialogue* the word *encounter* should be used. This word might also show the direction in which to find the most creative ways of being together.

October 1995

Sunday, October 1

During my farewell celebration at the Dayspring, two large blue candles were presented to me, one for me to take on my journey, and one to go from house to house in the community. They are prayer candles and are meant to remind me and those who sent me of our commitment to each other.

I realize how often my candle is burning! When I write my candle is lit to help make my writing a way of praying, and when I pray the candle is lit to connect me with my friends at home.

Community is so much more than living and working together. It is a bond of the heart that has no physical limitations. Indeed it is candles burning in different places of the world, all praying the same silent prayer of friendship and love.

Wednesday, October 4

At 3:00 p.m. this afternoon, Pope John Paul II arrived at Newark Airport to begin his five-day visit to the United States. I watched his arrival on television and listened to the speeches by President Clinton and the Pope.

From all the words spoken, one sentence by Pope John Paul stuck in my mind: "Nobody is so poor that he has nothing to give, and nobody is so rich that he has nothing to receive." That is a powerful idea to undergird all peacemaking. As long as we keep dividing people or nations between those who give and those who receive, there will always be oppression and manipulation, even with the best intentions. The United States is a powerful nation that has much to give. But only if it is also willing to receive can its giving be a true contribution to peace.

Among the many dignitaries I saw Cardinal Bernardin. I was glad to see that he had been able to make the trip from Chicago to welcome John Paul II. His pancreatic cancer must be under control and his energy sufficient to participate in this tiring event.

I am looking forward to watching tomorrow morning's broadcast of the Pope's address to the United Nations on its fiftieth anniversary. I still have vivid memories of watching — while on vacation in Mexico City with my parents — Pope Paul VI's visit to the UN, where he spoke these memorable words: "No more war, never war again." That was in 1965. Now, thirty years later, after many more wars, another Pope comes to the same place, with the same message. Will it ever happen: a world without wars?

Thursday, October 5

Pope John Paul's address to the United Nations struck me by its great spiritual vision. He spoke about the accelerated quest for freedom all around the world, freedom not only for individuals but for nations as well. He discussed this quest for freedom as an essential element of the inner structure of the human person. Reminding his listeners of the year 1989, when freedom was brought about in Eastern Europe without violence, he stressed the fact that in many places in our world this freedom is still a faraway goal. At the end of his address he unfolded a vision for the recuperation of the Transcendent as needed to attain the full freedom that people and nations are hungry for.

For me it was a very moving address. It was offered by a man who truly has lived much, seen much, and still has the courage to offer a spiritual vision that will allow all the people of this world to live together as brothers and sisters. In a society so full of cynicism and realpolitik, there are few leaders who can give the way John Paul II can. It is no surprise that millions of people from the most divergent social and economic backgrounds want to catch a glimpse of or, better, a blessing from this holy peacemaker.

Sunday, October 8

This morning, I drove to the home of my longtime friend Jutta. After an hour's drive on the nearly empty highways, I arrived at Jutta's home at 9:00 a.m. Together we celebrated the Eucharist in her living room, reflecting on the readings and sharing the divine gifts of life.

Monday, October 9

I watched the Pope's departure from the Baltimore-Washington Airport on television and was more deeply moved than I expected to be. I sometimes find it hard to feel connected with all the fanfare, choreographed ceremonies, mass rallies, and overall hype that characterize a papal visit. When I see the cardinals, bishops, and civil dignitaries crowding around the Pope, and the thousands of people trying to shake his hand, touch his white cassock, or just catch a glimpse of him, I create some inner distance from it all, as if it is a spectacle that has little to do with my life and my concerns.

But as I watched several of the events and listened carefully to what John Paul II was saying, there gradually emerged for me a spiritual vision greater, wiser, and more encompassing than any other vision I have seen in our contemporary world. The Pope's vision includes the human quest for freedom, the rights of individuals and nations, the religious importance of ecumenism and interreligious dialogue, the importance of the family, the sacredness of life from conception to natural death, and the true meaning of democracy. I saw that vision unfold as the Pope spoke to the civil and religious leaders; to men and women of the most diverse cultural and economic backgrounds; to the elderly, the young people, and to the children; to policemen, security guards, airplane pilots, and stewards.

Watching him during his five-day visit, I gradually got in touch with his vision, a vision that is universal, all-inclusive, rooted in a deep knowledge of God's love, inspired by the Gospel of Jesus, and rich in concrete implications for our daily lives. I was moved that this septuagenarian leader had a language that could speak to the most secular as well as to the most religious person, that this vision has no sectarian narrowness while it is fully based on the teachings of Jesus. It is a vision for all people and embraces all of creation. It is a demanding vision, yet full of compassion; it is a comforting vision, yet full of gentleness; it is a critical vision, yet full of understanding. It is a vision, as the *New York Times* says, that defies political labeling. It opposes abortion and euthanasia while stressing the urgency to care for the poor, to show compassion to the sick and the dying, especially those with AIDS, and to welcome immigrants generously. The words *conservative* and *liberal* do not fit such a vision.

Reflecting on this vision, I realize that the Pope was doing much more than offering his opinions on things. He spoke not for himself but in the Name of God, as revealed through Jesus. His words, although influenced by particular philosophies and theologies, are embedded in a tradition of Christian faith that is twenty centuries old.

It is very hard to know where time-bound opinions and a timeless vision need to be distinguished. Who can even fully know where personal opinions are presented as eternal truth and where eternal truth is truly eternal? As the centuries have rolled by, much that once seemed eternal has proven very temporal, and much that seemed very temporal has been revealed as having eternal significance. We have to trust that in the midst of the many ideas and statements there is a vision undergirding them all.

John Paul II has strong opinions with which many people disagree. The many controversies in the church concerning the role of women, sexual ethics, and the exercise of authority show clearly that there is a lot to discuss and to reflect on. I guess that many of John Paul II's ideas will be rethought and reformulated during the decades to come. But beyond all opinions, he proclaims a vision that is more than personal, a vision that is divinely inspired and transcends human speculation and debate. It is this vision that I saw emerging during the papal visit. It is a true catholic — that is, universal — vision, a vision this world so much needs as we enter the next millennium.

Friday, October 13

. . . Tomorrow I am leaving for six days. On Sunday and Monday I am going to be with my friends Wendy and Jay, and with Fred and Robin in New York. On Tuesday I plan to take the train to Philadelphia to visit another friend, Steve, and on Wednesday I will return to New York and spend some time with my publishers there. I am looking forward to this little trip. I will take my journal and my little notebook for daily reflections with me. I hope that after these weeks of relative solitude, this trip to friends will give me new inspiration and new energy.

Sunday, October 15

This afternoon at three o'clock Wendy and I went to a Gustav Mahler concert at Carnegie Hall. The program consisted of the "Kindertotenlieder" and the Sixth Symphony. The orchestra was the Metropolitan Opera Orchestra, the conductor, James Levine, and the soloist, the bass-baritone Bryn Terfel, a native of North Wales.

Many weeks ago Wendy had invited me to go with her to this unique event. It was an unforgettable experience. Just being at Carnegie Hall for the first time was a real treat.

I had never heard Mahler's "Kindertotenlieder." They are based on poems by the German poet Friedrich Rückert (1788–1866), written as an expression of grief at the death, from scarlet fever, of his children Louise and Ernst in January 1833. Gustav Mahler, who had grieved deeply over the loss of his fourteen-year-old brother, Ernst, set to music five of Rückert's "Songs on the Death of Children."

I was deeply moved by the performance and wished that Margaret and Jonas could have been there. Their grief over the loss of their daughter, Rebecca, who died only a few hours after her birth, found such a powerful expression in Mahler's music. They would have cried many tears.

After the intermission, Levine directed the Sixth Symphony. It is considered one of Mahler's greatest works and expresses a great range of emotion — exuberant joy, intense anguish, pastoral serenity, great pain, sadness, fear, hope, and despair. Everything is intense, elaborate, and majestic. The orchestra was the largest I had ever seen. During the eighty-one-minute performance, I mostly looked — with Wendy's binoculars — at the percussion section. There were seven men moving from one instrument to the other, trying to keep up with the various sounds they had to produce. For certain periods, I became so fascinated by their actions and interactions that I forgot to listen to the music. These men in gray suits and ties looked dead serious, in stark contrast to the joyful noises they were making. Especially one man with a strikingly beautiful, deeply carved face and long black hair, handling the large brass cymbals, who went about his business without the slightest change of expression. While looking at these figures, I started to wonder what their lives looked like outside of Carnegie Hall or Lincoln Center.

When it was over the applause was long and enthusiastic. New Yorkers are spoiled and seldom applaud for very long. But this was an exception....

Monday, October 16

Today Fred and I had a delightful walk in Central Park and lunch. At 6:00 p.m. I went to Fred's home to spend some time with Robin, his wife, and their two children, three-and-a-half-year-old Jacob and their newborn baby, Emma. A real joy. During dinner we talked about books, mutual work, friends, and future plans. A good and peaceful evening!

Philadelphia, Tuesday, October 17

Today I spent the day in Philadelphia with my friend Steve. For seventeen years Steve was an assistant bank manager in the City of Brotherly Love, and then he decided to go to seminary. He had saved up enough money to dedicate himself to the study of theology and to discern his call to the ministry.

This is not an easy time for Steve. The change from bank life to seminary life is very demanding on him. Although he enjoys his studies very much, he regrets that he has so little time left for personal reading, art, and mostly friendship.

Moreover he has to go through many hoops: psychological testing, psychotherapy, and endless interviews to qualify as a candidate for ministry. Listening to him I realized that I would never have made it to my ordination if I had been subjected, in my time, to the battery of tests they are subjecting Steve to today.

We talked long hours about vocation, competency, church work, future possibilities, and so on. Most important to me was that Steve is very glad to have left his bank job and loves his studies. What will come from it is hard to say. I kept saying, "Be sure that you love the life you're living now, your studies, your prayers, your friendships.... Then you can trust that God will reveal to you the direction to go when the time comes. But don't try to know now what you only have to know a few years from now."

I hope and pray that I can be of support to Steve in the years ahead. Steve took a risk by embarking on a road he doesn't know much about. But I feel that it is a beautifully inspired risk, worth taking. I am grateful that Steve put his trust in God, and not in a secure but basically unsatisfying job. I am convinced that one day his decision will bear many fruits.

New York, Wednesday, October 18

... When I returned to Wendy and Jay's apartment, Wendy said, "I bought two tickets for *Carmen*, tonight at the Metropolitan Opera. Jay and Jon are both out tonight, and I thought we could see *Carmen* together." I was delighted since I had never seen *Carmen*, and going to the Met was certainly the best possible introduction to this famous piece of music, song, and drama.

Although I went with the prejudice that operas are most often a combination of good music and a bad story, I became completely absorbed by the drama of *Carmen*. Carmen was sung and acted by Denyce Graves. Her portrayal of the sensual, seductive, self-confident, fatalistic gypsy woman opened up in me the real tension between faith and fate, the obedient life and the "wild" life, agape and eros, and Christianity and paganism.

In *Carmen*, José, the Spanish soldier in Seville who has to obey his military superiors and cannot let "love" distract him, stands for many of us dutiful men and women who feel that life kills our vitality. Carmen's irresistible energy enlarges José's life but finally, destroying them both, represents us as people who want to break away from the constraints of normalcy but hesitate to pay the price.

Can the tension be resolved in an integrated life? Can the "wild person" in us be tamed without the cost of losing our vitality and creativity? Many forms of meditation, Buddhist as well as Christian, strive for this integration. I do not believe that we have to repress our erotic energies in order to live or-dered lives. Nor do I believe that we have to give up order and discipline in order to get in touch with the wild energies of ex-istence. But it certainly requires concentrated effort to find our own unique ways to become whole people. The literature and art of the West show that few have accomplished this whole-ness. I certainly have not. I don't know what would happen if a Carmen barged into my life and swept me off my feet.

Watertown, Thursday, October 19

An in-between day! I am between the exciting time in New York and a promising weekend in Boston.

Tomorrow Nathan and Sue will come for the weekend. They are coming as friends but also as accompaniers, helping me to live my sabbatical well. I am looking forward to their visit. I'd better get everything ready! I have to buy food, get the apartment in shape, and plan with Jonas and Margaret the details of their stay.

A great and happy surprise is that Borys, with whom Nathan, Sue, and I spent several weeks in Ukraine, happens to be in Boston and will join us all tomorrow morning. There will be a lot to talk about.

Friday, October 20

This afternoon at 4:00, Jonas, Margaret, Sam, Jonas's brother Steve, Steve's six-year-old, Luke, and I went to the circus.

I was very happy for the opportunity to see the Ringling Brothers, Barnum & Bailey "Greatest Show on Earth," since my more than four-year-old friendship with the trapeze group the Flying Rodleighs has made me a great circus fan.

For me the three-ring circus of Ringling Brothers, Barnum & Bailey, where so much is going on at the same time, prevents any kind of personal relationship with the performers. They are reduced from very talented people to spectacular movements and colorful forms. I missed the intimacy of the one-ring tent circus of Simoneit-Barum in Germany. When I saw the Flying Rodleighs there, I was moved not only by their aerial act but also by their spirits. I wanted to know them personally and become more intimately connected with their lives. This afternoon I was impressed, overwhelmed, awestruck, et cetera, but never really moved. I was forced to forget that these people in front of me were human beings like I am. They had become parts of a huge magic machine called the circus.

I wondered how Sam and Luke would respond to it. They sat with glazed eyes looking at it all, but they never laughed or got excited. Sam crawled onto Margaret's lap and said that he was tired. I don't blame him!

There was one moment when I got "caught." It was when one man performed a one-armed handstand on the head of his partner, who kept two freestanding stilts in balance on a platform thirty feet above the arena floor. I could see them so well because our seats were right in front of their act. I could see the first man's open, smiling face and his straining, muscular body, which radiated so much vitality and energy. I felt a connection. But then they vanished in the large anonymity of the show. It was an important moment for me though, short as it was, because I recognized within me the same emotion that caught me when I first saw the Flying Rodleighs. It was the emotion that made me take the risk of introducing myself to them and that has led to a long and rich friendship. This act and the men performing it were like a flash of light in the darkness, a recognition, a memory, and an inner connection full of melancholy.

Wednesday, October 25

The fiftieth anniversary of the United Nations is bringing many of the political leaders of the world to the United States. The sensitivities are complex, protocol nearly unmanageable, security a nightmare, transportation causing long delays, and accommodations overbooked. The overall mood seems quite pessimistic. The UN, after fifty years, has become a huge bureaucracy without much vision, bogged down in endless diplomatic problems. Still, it is one of the few organizations that has the potential for creating peace on our planet and preventing it from being destroyed by human greed and revenge.

Compared with all the diplomatic maneuvering this week, Pope John Paul II's visit a few weeks ago seems like an unusually prophetic event.

I pray for world peace tonight.

Thursday, October 26

A full day of writing: five short reflections about being a wounded healer, a chapter in the cup book on lifting up your life for others, and a five-page meditation on unconditional love for my friend Joan, in San Diego. At 6:00 p.m. Borys appeared for dinner and talked about his busy time in Cambridge trying to finish his book and meet several people before returning to Europe.

Friday, October 27

Most of this day I spent working on the foreword to Jonas's book, *Rebecca: A Father's Journey from Grief to Gratitude.* Yesterday I had a short "interview" with Jonas, and this morning I wrote the text. I was very glad to make this little contribution to Jonas's first book, especially since I feel so connected with Jonas and with his grief for Rebecca, who was born prematurely on July 29, 1992. She lived three hours and forty-four minutes and then died in Jonas's arms. At that time I was in France. I still remember Jonas telling me by phone about Rebecca's birth and death. His grief was immense, but his willingness to let his pain lead him to gratitude was there also from the very beginning.

Later I suggested to Jonas that he write about Rebecca. He had always hoped to be a writer. Rebecca's short life, I said, could make him one. It is such a joy to see the fruit of deep grief and the product of hard work.

What struck me most was that this book can be read in two ways. It can be read as the senseless attempt of a father trying at all costs to give meaning to a meaningless event. But it can also be read as a glorious witness to the mystery that we are citizens of heaven, from where we expect our Savior, the Lord Jesus Christ, to transform the body of our humiliation into the body of his glory (see Phil 3:20–21). When one chooses, with Jonas, to see God's glory in the midst of the immense human grief, this book can truly give great hope.

Rebecca lived only three hours and forty-four minutes. She was too fragile, too little to open her eyes. But Jonas's great spiritual vision allowed him to see that the value of life is not dependent on the hours, days, or years it is lived, nor on the number of people it was connected to, nor on the impact it had on human history. Jonas "saw" that the value of life is life itself and that the few hours of Rebecca's life were as worthy to be lived as the many hours of the lives of Beethoven, Chagall, Gandhi, yes, even Jesus. . . .

November 1995

Cancún, Mexico, Monday, November 6

At 7:00 a.m. I watched the funeral of Premier Rabin on CNN. A deeply moving sight. Political leaders from all over the world were present. I pray that Yitzhak Rabin's violent death will bring a new unity to Israel and give a new momentum to peace in the Middle East. I think about Jesus' words "Unless a grain of wheat falls into the earth and dies, it remains just a single grain; but if it dies, it bears much fruit" (Jn 12:24). As I saw the deep grief of Rabin's wife, Leah, and his children and granddaughter, I was hoping that their tears will become like rain on the barren desert, making it bloom with new life.

Watertown, Friday, November 10

As I started to write again today, I realized that The Gathering [a support network for philanthropists] had raised new questions in my mind about mission, evangelization, conversion, witness, and so on. Many of the people I met in Cancún believe that without an explicit personal profession of faith in Jesus as our Lord and Savior, we cannot make it to heaven.

They are convinced that God has called us to convert every human being to Jesus.

This vision inspires much generosity, commitment, and a great worldwide project. Not a few of the men and women we met had traveled far and wide, put their lives and health in danger, given large parts of their personal income, and taken many financial risks. Their love for Jesus is deep, intense, and radical. They spoke about Jesus fearlessly and were prepared for rejection and ridicule. They are very committed disciples, not hesitant to pay the cost of their discipleship.

Still ... I felt somewhat uncomfortable, even though this belief was present in my own upbringing. My conviction as a young man was that there is no salvation outside the Catholic Church and that it was my task to bring all "nonbelievers" into the one true church.

But much has happened to me over the years. My own psychological training, my exposure to people from the most different religious backgrounds, the Second Vatican Council, the new theology of mission, and my life in L'Arche have all deepened and broadened my views on Jesus' saving work. Today I personally believe that while Jesus came to open the door to God's house, all human beings can walk through that door, whether they know about Jesus or not. Today I see it as my call to help every person claim his or her own way to God. I feel deeply called to witness for Jesus as the one who is the source of my own spiritual journey and thus create the possibility for other people to know Jesus and commit themselves to him. I am so truly convinced that the Spirit of God is present in our midst and that each person can be touched by God's Spirit in ways far beyond my own comprehension and intention.

I am using my little daily reflections to articulate my own theology of evangelization, mission, salvation, and redemption. I am very grateful for my time at The Gathering. It forces me to think through my own religious convictions.

Sunday, November 19

The Eucharist this morning with Jonas and his prayer group at the Empty Bell was very vibrant and alive.

In the Gospel Jesus says, "Beware that you are not led astray; for many will come in my name and say, 'I am he!' and 'The time is near!' Do not go after them.... Nation will rise against nation, and kingdom against kingdom ... there will be dreadful portents.... They will arrest you and persecute you. ... This will give you an opportunity to testify. So make up your minds not to prepare your defense in advance; for I will give you words and a wisdom that none of your opponents will be able to withstand or contradict.... You will be hated by all because of my name. But not a hair of your head will perish. By your endurance you will gain your souls" (Lk 21:8–19).

What a powerful and hopeful word! Life with all its turmoil is an opportunity to witness to God's love! And our witness will be irresistible when we realize that God keeps us completely safe.

The many events of life so easily pull us in all directions and make us lose our souls. But when we remain anchored in the heart of God, rooted in God's love, we have nothing to fear, not even death, and everything joyful and everything painful will give us a chance to proclaim the Kingdom of Jesus.

Different people in the circle spoke and shared their faith and their hope. Then we prayed together and received the Body and Blood of Jesus. We are called to be fearless people in a fearful world.

Monday, November 20

A very quiet, peaceful day. Writing, reading, going to the health club with Jonas, sleeping, and making some phone calls.

One of the calls was to a longtime friend, Timothy, who is married to Phyllis and who has three young children. He is a religion teacher at a Catholic high school and an accomplished guitarist and singer, and he has written many liturgical songs with his friend Paul. He loves Jesus, Mary, and the saints, and he is a man filled with the Spirit of God.

About a year ago Timothy was told that he had liver cancer, and so he started chemotherapy. Now he is quite weak and wonders how long he has to live. Recently he made a pilgrimage to Lourdes with Phyllis. He found much hope and courage there to live this illness as part of his spiritual journey.

It was so good to talk to Tim again. He is such a man of faith. In the midst of all his suffering he speaks about his illness as a "privilege," a grace from God, a blessing calling him closer to the heart of Jesus. No sentimentality, no sweet piety, but deep, strong faith. When he speaks about Jesus and Mary, his voice brims over with love and gratitude.

What a saintly man! What a joy to have him as a friend!

Wednesday, November 22

This morning the local florist brought a beautiful flower arrangement. It was a Thanksgiving greeting from my friend Joan. Besides some large sunflowers, there were some shining apples in the piece. I feel happy to be remembered and grateful for friendship.

A little card was added by the florist saying, "Do not eat the fruit!" Was this a reminder of paradise? It made me think of Adam and Eve in the Garden of Eden.

Tonight Jutta is coming, and she, Jonas, my friend Vincent, and I are going to listen to Bernard Haitink conduct the Boston Symphony in Mozart and Ravel. I am very much looking forward to it. Tomorrow is Thanksgiving Day.

Thanksgiving, Thursday, November 23

Today I am staying home to write, pray, and rest. I wondered whether I should join a friend for Thanksgiving dinner, but I finally realized that the best thing for me to do would be to be quietly at home. Jonas, Margaret, and Sam left for a few days in Vermont, so I am alone in the big house. I enjoy the immense quiet, no lawn mowers, shouting kids, or garbage trucks, just complete silence.

Friday, November 24

Jean Vanier often told me that I should write about the church, but I never have, at least not directly. I always have experienced a deep inner resistance to writing about the church because it seemed like a field full of thorn bushes. I guess I fear that I will become entrapped, and for that reason I have been avoiding it until today.

After writing several reflections about baptism and the Eucharist, I spontaneously started to write about the church as the community of people fashioned by these two sacraments. Once I entered the subject that way, I discovered there was a lot to think about and reflect upon.

I love the church. I do not want to write about the church as a problem, a source of conflict, a place of controversies, but as the Body of Christ for us here and now.

Sunday, November 26

The Feast of Christ the King. On the last Sunday of the liturgical year, Christ is presented to us as the mocked King on the cross as well as the King of the universe. The greatest humiliation and the greatest victory are both shown to us in today's liturgy.

It is important to look at this humiliated and victorious Christ before we start the new liturgical year with the celebration of Advent. All through the year we have to stay close to the humiliation as well as to the victory of Christ, because we are called to live both in our own daily lives. We are small *and* big, specks in the universe *and* the glory of God, little fearful people *and* sons and daughters of the Lord of all creation.

Tuesday, November 28

Last night I got stuck in my writing. I was trying to reflect on the resurrection of Jesus and on our resurrection. I reflected myself into a corner, not knowing how to articulate that, on the one hand, our bodies will return to "dust" while, on the other hand, nothing we have lived in the body will go to waste.

When I sat down to write again this morning, I didn't know where to go with my thoughts. Then I saw that Paul raises my very question when he asks rhetorically, "How are dead people raised, and what sort of body do they have?" He answers with unwavering conviction, "How foolish! What you sow must die before it is given new life, and what you sow is not the body that is to be, but only a bare grain, of wheat I dare say, or some other kind; it is God who gives it the sort of body that he has chosen for it" (1 Cor 15:35–38).

This answer really woke me up! It was as if I heard it for the very first time. Our life is a seed that has to die to be dressed with immortality! Things suddenly came together and started to make sense, spiritual sense. From then on my pen could hardly stop moving.

◆ ◆ ◆

When I called Kathy this morning, she told me that Carrie and Geoff, members of Daybreak and dear friends, had their baby, David Friend; he was born last night at 7:00. A healthy boy, a brother for Janet and Monica, a new joy for everyone in the community.

At 3:30 p.m. Kathy called to tell me that Robin, former director of Daybreak, married to Joan and father of Emily, Laura, and Elaine, had been hospitalized with a serious heart problem. I immediately tried to reach Joan, which wasn't possible. Then I called Joe to get some more information. Joe said that Robin's condition is serious and told me he would call when he knew more.

How fragile is life. I pray for David Friend and Robin. May God embrace them both in tender love.

Wednesday, November 29

When I started to write my reflections for every day of the year, I had no outline or plan. I simply wrote what came to mind on the day I was writing. In the beginning I wrote about things I have written about often before. But as I continued I found myself choosing subjects that I never thought I would write about, such as baptism, the Eucharist, the church, the resurrection, heaven and hell. Very basic themes. Today I wrote about hell! After having written so much about God's love, God's mercy, God's all-embracing kindness, I found my-self faced with strong words about hell. When I read the beautiful words about the New Heaven and the New Earth in the Book of Revelation, I also came across the words "the legacy for cowards, for those who break their word, or worship obscenities, for murderers and the sexually immoral, and for sorcerers, worshippers of false gods or any other sort of liars, is the second death in the burning lake of sulphur" (Rev 21:8).

Just as there is an eternal life, there is an eternal death, the second death. Hell is eternal death. Is this a possibility for me, for us? I felt a real resistance in me to saying yes to that question, but Jesus and his apostles give me no way out here. Eternal death is as possible as eternal life! God offers us a choice. To say yes or no to love. To offer me a choice is to respect me as a free human person. I am no robot or automaton who has no choice. God, who loves me in freedom, wants my love in freedom. That means that no is a possibility. Eternal life is not a predetermined fact. It is the fruit of our human response.

Thursday, November 30

When I called Kathy at 1:30 p.m. she told me that Conrad, my former editor in Toronto, had died this morning.

December 1995

Friday, December 1

The most important event of this day was finishing my reflections for every day of the year. I filled my last museum notebook today with number 387. Although even in a leap year there are only 366 days, I wrote some extra meditations that can be used in place of those that are repetitive or poorly written....

Sunday, December 3

This morning we celebrated the first Sunday of Advent at the Empty Bell. All together we were twenty-two people. It was a peaceful and joyful celebration. There was a feeling of friendship, mutual care, and spiritual unity. Jonas creates a truly safe and holy place for the people who come. I hope they will keep coming after my departure. This was my last Eucharist at the Empty Bell. I am grateful that I could be such an intimate part of Jonas's ministry.

Monday, December 4

This afternoon Kathy called and told me about Conrad's funeral. She said, "There were nearly as many priests on the altar as there were people in the church. It was an intimate and beautiful service."

I wish I could have been there. Often during the weekend I thought about Conrad. Life is so short! Carrie and Geoff just had their baby. Kathy, another Daybreak friend, is expecting a baby, and so are Alan and Judy. Conrad dies, Tim is dying.

How much longer will I live? Quite a few of my classmates have died already. But my father is nearly ninety-three and in good spirits. I could live another thirty years! Do I want to live that long? Or do I hope to be united with Christ sooner?

Only one thing seems clear to me. Every day should be well lived. What a simple truth! Still, it is worth my attention. Did I offer peace today? Did I bring a smile to someone's face? Did I say words of healing? Did I let go of my anger and resentments? Did I forgive? Did I love? These are the real questions! I must trust that the little bit of love that I sow now will bear many fruits, here in this world and in the life to come. . . .

Tuesday, December 5

I just finished reading one of the most riveting books I have read in a long time, Alan Helms's *Young Man from the Provinces*. The subtitle is *A Gay Life before Stonewall*. Few people have seen so much, met so many, and "played" so hard. Everything is here: abuse, sex, drugs, fame, money, travel, books, films, theater, and a long, long list of famous men and women. And what is the conclusion?

In his epilogue Helms writes, "I learned a few things. . . . I learned that being envied is the loneliest pleasure on earth, that self-absorption guarantees unhappiness, that the worst motive for action is groundless fear. And I wouldn't cross the street these days to meet someone who's merely celebrated or rich. I've seen so many of those people up close that I know how little such things count for in the effort to make a good life."

If ever I got a gut sense of the journey from entrapment to freedom, it was from this book.

I will send Alan Helms a copy of *The Return of the Prodigal Son*. He might never read it, but it makes me feel good to send it in gratitude for his "confession."

Peapack, New Jersey, Thursday, December 7

A lovely day. Peggy welcomed me at Newark Airport and took me to her beautiful home in Peapack.

She had invited four guests for dinner. Also Andrew, Peggy's youngest son, came from New York to join us. We had an animated discussion about the Catholic Church, being a Christian, and family values. Peggy made sure to keep the conversation from moving to small talk. She wanted us to have a real discussion about significant things. What a great friend she is, full of humor, vitality, and love. I asked her whether I could stay with her in February, after I return from Holland. She was excited about the idea and offered me her "barn house," which stands separate from her large home. It is an ideal place to have solitude and to write. I am really looking forward to making Peapack my residence for the winter, spring, and summer.

New York, Friday, December 8

At 10:30 I left to have lunch in New York with Jim and Margaret and talk about their marriage tomorrow. Jim is Jutta's son. Since I had never met Margaret and only saw Jim at his sister's wedding a few years ago, I wanted to know them a little better before preaching at their wedding. We had a very open and honest conversation. . . .

Saturday, December 9

What can I write about Jim and Margaret's wedding? It was beautiful, solemn, colorful, and consciously medieval. There was the Cathedral of St. John the Divine, one of the largest churches in the world, majestic, high, deep, in many ways overwhelming. The ceremony took place in front of the main altar, with the guests sitting in the choir stalls. There were the ushers and the bridesmaids, young, exquisitely dressed, good looking, self-assured New York businessmen and women. There was the choir of St. John the Divine, boys and girls with red cassocks and white surplices. There were many candles and flowers. There was a splendid organ filling the space with Bach's music. John, the Episcopal priest presiding, led us with grace.

In the homily I told Jim and Margaret, their families and friends, that I had gone this morning to the Metropolitan Museum to see Arnold Böcklin's painting *Island of the Dead* because it was this painting that Margaret and Jim saw and admired on their first date. It speaks of darkness and light, death and life, and "unglamorous glamour." I simply asked them, "How are you going to live your mutual love in a world of unglamorous glamour?" My answer was this: "Your love for each other comes from God's first love. Keep claiming that love. Your love for each other is a forgiving love. Keep talking to each other, pardoning each other's shortcomings and praising each other's gifts. Your love for each other is for others, your children, your guests, the poor. Keep your attention focused on those who need to be nurtured by your love." At the conclusion I gave them a framed reproduction of Rembrandt's etching *Three Trees*, saying that they are two, but there is always a Third who is with them, guiding them through the valley of death whether they see it and know it or not.

Watertown, Tuesday, December 12

My time with Jonas, Margaret, and Sam is coming to an end. In one week's time I will be on my way to Holland. Tomorrow is my last day in the apartment, because Sarah returns on Friday. It is such a wonderful space to live in. I will miss it a lot.

Monday, December 18

This is a day of unpacking and packing, Christmas shopping, writing letters, sending gifts, making phone calls, and planning to get ready for my departure to Holland tomorrow night.

Geysteren, Holland, Thursday, December 21

My nephew Reinier was at the airport to take me to my father's home in Limburg, a two-hour ride. The first thing my ninety-three-year-old father said was, "Well, you badly need a haircut." I will make an appointment with the barber for both of us, so we will look decent on our trip! Then he said, "You better go to bed right away, so you can catch up with your sleep." A father is always a father!

Friday, December 22

Getting ready! Going to the barber! Sleeping! Packing! Making phone calls! Tonight my sister, Laurien, and her partner,

Henri, came to say hello, and we all went to Horst, a nearby small town, for dinner.

Freiburg, Germany, Saturday, December 23

... At 9:00 a.m. [my father] was all set to go on the trip and hardly mentioned his stomach troubles. Joe, a friend and distant relative of my father, drove us to Venlo, where we caught the train to Cologne. At noon we left Cologne, and at 4:00 p.m. we arrived in Freiburg. Franz was at the station and drove us to a small, intimate hotel close to the Münster (Freiburg's cathedral). While my father rested, I made a quick trip with Franz to his home to greet Reny, his wife, and pick up two suitcases with clothes and books I had left there two years ago. After a good meal at the hotel, my father and I retired to our rooms. I am feeling very tired.

Sunday, December 24

At 9:30 p.m. Franz and Reny came to the hotel to take me to the Christmas mass at their parish church. My father, who had stomach problems again, decided to stay at the hotel and go to bed early.

I was surprised to see that the church was far from full. I am so used to the overcrowded services in Richmond Hill that I expected the same here. But it was a rather small "crowd."

The pastor welcomed us warmly and invited me to concelebrate with him. The assistant pastor gave a lovely reflection about God's desire to move from power to powerlessness, from strength to weakness, from being creator to being creative, from greatness to smallness, from independence to dependence.

It brought me back to my musings earlier this week. I think that we have hardly thought through the immense implications of the mystery of the incarnation. Where is God? God is where we are weak, vulnerable, small, and dependent. God is where the poor are, the hungry, the handicapped, the mentally ill, the elderly, the powerless. How can we come to know God when our focus is elsewhere, on success, influence, and power? I increasingly believe that our faithfulness will depend on our willingness to go where there is brokenness, loneliness, and human need. If the church has a future, it is a future with the poor in whatever form. Each one of us is very seriously searching to live and grow in this belief, and by friendship we can support each other. I realize that the only way for us to stay well in the midst of the many "worlds" is to stay close to the small, vulnerable child that lives in our hearts and in every other human being. Often we do not know that the Christ child is within us. When we discover him we can truly rejoice.

Christmas, Monday, December 25

Shortly before 10:00 a.m. my father and I took a cab to the cathedral (Das Münster). It was packed, but I was able to get my father a seat in the front row, which was reserved for the elderly. The service was festive, solemn, and very "royal" — processions, incense, candles, and many servers.

The archbishop of Freiburg presided and gave the homily. "Does this cathedral help or hinder us in understanding the mystery of Christmas?" he asked. I was fascinated by the question, since I had just been thinking about the fact that such a hidden and poor event as the birth of Jesus had inspired the creation of such a majestic building and such a rich liturgy. What had all the Gothic splendor, the paintings and sculptures, the robes, staff, miter, and long ceremonies to do with the little baby born in Bethlehem twenty centuries ago?

The bishop "defended" his cathedral, but afterward my father said, "He has a very optimistic view of human nature. He didn't mention all the human evil that causes so much suffering in our world." I realized that perhaps the cathedral is as much a product of human pride, arrogance, and desire for power, influence, and success as it is of deep faith, piety, adoration, generosity, and the love of God. The Freiburg Münster is one of the best places to see in stone the place where power and piety meet.

I had a splendid view of the majestic church. It is without any doubt one of the most beautiful Gothic churches ever erected. It took five centuries to build. In November 1944 the city of Freiburg and most of the cathedral were destroyed by Allied bombing. Happily the unique cathedral tower, with its beautiful filigreed spire, was spared. It took more than twenty years to restore the cathedral to its present glory.

74

Tuesday, December 26

At 11:00 a.m. an influential priest in the diocese came to the hotel for a visit, and I was moved by our conversation. He was very honest about his feelings concerning being a prominent member of the church hierarchy while being mostly interested in the spiritual formation of religious and laypeople. During the week he is quite busy with the administration of the diocese, but on the weekend he escapes to a spiritual center an hour away from the city to spend time in prayer and solitude. He is a kind, warm, open-minded person, with an obvious love for Jesus and the church. But he also realizes that high liturgies, miters, purple cassocks, lots of incense, and clerical formality are no longer speaking to young people in search of meaning.

This priest reflects my own struggle to be in the church without being caught in many complicated structures. The question for him as well as for me is, how can we love the church today? He said to me, "I am always happy when I can get out of my purple robes and look like a normal person again." But then he went on to say, "I have to live day by day, be faithful to my call, and trust that my life will be fruitful, even when things don't change as fast as I would like." I really liked this simple, honest man of the church.

◆ ◆ ◆

This afternoon I wrote many postcards. While writing I experienced a deep love for all the friends I was writing to. My heart was full of gratitude and affection, and I wished I could embrace each of my friends and let them know how much they mean to me and how much I miss them. It seems that sometimes distance creates closeness, absence creates presence, loneliness creates community! I felt my whole being, body, mind, and spirit, yearning to give and receive love without condition, without fear, without reservation.

Why should I ever think or say something that is not love? Why should I ever hold a grudge, feel hatred or jealousy, act suspiciously? Why not always give and forgive, encourage and empower, give thanks and offer praise? Why not?

I thank God for this little glimpse of eternity in my own heart. I pray that I can hold on to the truth of what my spiritual eye sees and find the strength to live my life according to that vision.

Wednesday, December 27

A very quiet day. There are many things to do and to see in Freiburg, but both my father and I enjoy just being here, with ample time to sleep, to have a relaxed breakfast, to celebrate the Eucharist, and to just rest. There were times when I could hardly be in a foreign city without wanting to see every church, every museum, and every ruin, but these days I am very satisfied to be in my room, read a little, write a little, and pray a little.

It is good for both my father and me to be together without any special agenda. I don't think that we ever before spent such unscheduled time together. We have no great subjects to discuss, but our conversations are alive and pleasant. I keep being surprised by my father's interest in religion, literature, art, and politics. Even though his body is worn out and he can hardly walk, his mind is as clear and sharp as ever, and his ideas, judgments, and opinions are to the point and often astute. For me it is a unique privilege to have this time with him, and I can see that he too is glad we are together.

At 5:00 p.m. Franz and Reny took us to the home of friends I came to know during my previous visits to Freiburg....

Thursday, December 28

Five years ago when my father and I were also together for a few days in Freiburg, we went to the circus, and during the performance I was so moved by the Flying Rodleighs, a group of South African trapeze artists, that I introduced myself to them. That little event had many consequences for me. I became friends with the Rodleighs, traveled with them through Germany, interviewed them at length, wrote articles about them, and made a documentary film with them, which will be shown on Dutch TV next Monday night, New Year's.

My father must have been thinking of the Rodleighs when he said, "There is a circus in town again. I wonder if you would like to go." It is the Christmas Circus Festival, a program with

77

the Chinese People's Circus and artists from Moscow, Paris, and Freiburg.

At 4:00 p.m. Franz, my father, and I drove to the great circus tent at the marketplace in Freiburg and saw the show. No animals, only acrobats! There were some dazzling jugglers, a fabulous wire dancer, a great cradle trapeze artist, and spectacular "teeter-totter" jumpers. But I was most fascinated by another act, with three men who combined clowning, dancing, and athletics accompanied by music from the film *Chariots of Fire*. There was much self-mockery in their act. While performing the most amazing athletics, they looked at the audience and at one another as if they were making fools of themselves. Hilarious.

But, spectacular as it was, nothing happened in me comparable to what happened five years ago. Then I was "hooked" by the Rodleighs and felt nearly driven to see them again and again and enter deeply into their world. Now I saw a good show and went home without many afterthoughts or afterfeelings. Then I saw something that opened in me a new inner place. Now I just enjoyed some unusual sights and had a few hours of good entertainment. Then I experienced a personal transformation.

Today's circus experience made it clear to me that what really had touched me last time was the very personal quality of the Rodleighs' trapeze act. I had been able to identify with the artists and came to think about them as people I'd like to become friends with. Indeed, they have become friends, and I have discovered the many ways my world and theirs interconnect. The people I saw today remained somewhat abstract to me. I wasn't curious about how they live their daily lives, as I was with the Rodleighs. I didn't think beyond their performance and forgot about them when it was over.

Friday, December 29

Today Franz took us on a little trip to Bernau, known for its wood-carving workshops, and to Sankt Blasien, known for its high-domed church. Most beautiful, however, was the trip itself, through the snow-covered Black Forest. It felt like driving through a very romantic Christmas card. The view into the valleys with their little villages and charming church towers, the winding roads, the white and green fir trees, and the heavy clouds moving between the hills and mountains was so pleasant to the eye from a well-heated Mercedes.

What I will probably most remember of our trip was a woman called Ursula. She was sitting alone in the restaurant where we went for lunch. When she noticed us she offered us a glass of red wine. I accepted her offer, and as a result she joined us a little later, obviously in need of company. Ursula is an astrologer who tried to convince us of the importance of her gifts to determine our personalities on the basis of the year, the day, and the minute of our birth. She spoke intensely, intrusively, and hardly gave us a chance to respond.

Soon she was busy attacking the Vatican, calling the Pope a poisonous influence, and telling us that she believed in God but had no use whatsoever for the church. She also declared that all the good Popes had been murdered, John Paul I being one of them, that the crusades, Inquisition, and pogroms showed how evil the church is, that Leonardo Boff was her hero, and that most theologians didn't know what they were talking about.

After listening to her tirade for ten minutes, I felt an unusually strong desire to put a needle in her balloon. So I looked her straight in the eyes, asked her to listen to me for a change, and told her that I was a Catholic priest, worked with handicapped people, had met the Pope himself, knew all about Leonardo Boff, and considered her tirade insensitive, simplistic, trendy, and very arrogant. I went on to say to her, "You are a person who has influence on people. What you say is important. Please mind that your words don't wound those you speak with, and please realize that the history of Christianity cannot be summarized in two or three condemnations."

Ursula fell completely silent. She hadn't expected such a strong response. She accepted my words as well as she could, asked me for my name, and wrote her name down for me. I am not sure if I did the right thing. Franz said, "I never heard you defend the Pope in such an unconditional way." I realized that Ursula's simplistic criticism of the church had made me a somewhat simplistic supporter. I don't think I was able to change her mind, but she certainly made me aware of my own mind!

Sunday, December 31

Tonight Hermann and Mechtilde invited us to celebrate "Silvester Evening," New Year's Eve, with their family. We started with the Eucharist in the living room. There were quite a few people. The liturgy was homey but also quite solemn. The most intimate part was the time of intercession, in which several members revealed their very personal concerns.

After the Eucharist we had a dinner à la bourguignon, in which each person could cook his own piece of meat in small pots of boiling oil and dip it in several sauces. It's the kind of meal that keeps you busy and encourages small talk.

At 10:00 p.m. a cab came to take my father and me back to the hotel. Soon after we got there the fireworks began, and they kept my father, whose room looks out on the square, awake for most of the night. On the garden side of the hotel, where my room is located, the New Year's noises weren't so bad, and I slept pretty well.

January 1996

Monday, January 1, 1996

After a very quiet and peaceful day in the hotel, we had a lovely farewell dinner with Franz and Reny, Hermann and Mechtilde. The manager of the hotel had done every possible thing to please us. The table was beautifully decorated, and for my father she had ordered a light meal.

The dinner was in honor of Hermann, who celebrates his seventieth birthday on January 17, and of my father, who celebrates his ninety-third on January 3. I had bought a silver letter opener for Hermann and an etching of the hotel square with the Schwabengate for my father. For Mechtilde I had a "consolation prize," a little bookmark in the form of an owl.

My father enjoyed himself very much and actively participated in these "cultural" discussions. It was truly a warm, charming, and intelligent conclusion to our Freiburg time.

Friday, January 5

During dinner Kathy called to let me know that my friend Timothy is dying. I immediately phoned Tim in Toronto and was amazed to be able to speak to him directly.

"The chemotherapy didn't work," he said. "Things only got worse." I asked him about his "spirits." He said, "There is much, much peace. Phyllis and I pray a lot together, and we have committed ourselves fully to Jesus and the blessed Mother." There was a certain joy in his voice, even though it was clear that he had become very weak.

I spoke also for a moment with Phyllis, his wife, and his dearest friend, Paul, who happened to be there when I called. I said to Phyllis, "I am so grateful that Tim has become part of my life. His deep faith and radical trust are a great inspiration to me, and I am sure that Tim's life will bear many, many fruits." She said, "Thank you so much for saying this. Your concern and interest means so much to Tim. I know that your call made his day." Paul said, "I'll keep you informed, but I don't think Tim can live longer than two weeks."

I have been thinking much about Tim since that call. His communion with God is so deep that all the pain, worries, and fears seem to recede into the background. Seldom if ever have I met a man who embraced his approaching death with so much love and so much confidence. What a grace to know this man!

Saturday, January 6

A very special day. The celebration of my father's ninety-third birthday! He had invited the entire immediate family: my brother Paul; my brother Laurent with his wife, Heiltjen, and their three children, Sarah, Laura, and Raphael; my sister, Laurien, with her companion, Henri, and her three children, Frédérique, Marc with his companion, Marije, and Reinier; and myself. Also present were my father's sister Hetty with her husband, Jan; his sisters Ella and Truus; Cathrien, the daughter of his deceased brother Sef, with her husband, Chris; Elisabeth, a friend of his deceased sister Corrie; and his relative Jo, who is his present driver and tour guide. Together we were twenty-two.

Since my father comes from a family of eleven children and my mother from a family of eight, this family reunion made us very conscious of the many members of our family who have died during the last years. My father asked me to celebrate the Eucharist in memory of my mother, who died eighteen years ago, and also in memory of all the other deceased members of the family.

We all sat around the living-room table in double rows. In sharp contrast to the liturgies I celebrate elsewhere, this was rather formal as many of the people present do not go to church. Sarah, Raphael, and Reinier did the readings. I felt that people seemed uncomfortable.

For me it is hard to celebrate the Eucharist in a formal or ritualistic way. I so much wish that we would feel more connected and inspired, but it seems that their spirituality and my own are miles apart. I spoke about God revealing himself to us in weakness, not only a long time ago in the birth of Jesus but also today wherever people are sick, elderly, dependent,

84

and out of control. I also said that we only live our weakness as a place of God's appearance (it was the day of Epiphany!) when we truly believe that we have been loved since before we were born and will be loved after we have died. If we do not believe this, our weakness easily leads to bitterness and hardened hearts. Although I felt deeply convinced of what I was talking about, my words did not seem to be very deeply received.

After the Eucharist we went to my mother's grave. We were reminded of that foggy morning in October 1978 when we walked from the church to the cemetery to lay her to rest. Most of us had been there, except for Sarah, Laura, and Raphael, who were all born after her death. How much she would have loved them!

The dinner at a nearby restaurant was quite festive. My brother Paul was master of ceremonies. Sarah spoke on behalf of the grandchildren, and both my sister, Laurien, and my brother Laurent offered humorous but affectionate reflections on my father's life and virtues.

During the dinner the local band walked in dressed up as kings to commemorate the Feast of the Three Kings, played "Happy Birthday" and a few other pieces, and passed the hat. A colorful musical interruption.

At 6:30 the dinner was over, and although the roads were very slippery, everyone made it to their cars and finally home!

◆ ◆ ◆

My time with my father in Germany and his ninety-third birthday will always stay with me as a precious memory. It is for me the best time we have ever had together. Maybe he had to be ninety-three and I had to be sixty-four to make this possible! Thirty years ago the closeness that now exists between us was unthinkable. Then it was my mother who offered closeness, affection, and personal care. My father seemed more distant. He was the provider who loved his wife, expected much of his children, worked hard, and discussed important issues. A virtuous, righteous man, but I found it difficult to feel intimate with him.

I realize that I have lived for a long time with a deep respect for, as well as a certain fear of, my father. When my mother died, I suddenly became aware that I hardly knew him. But as we both grew older and a little less defensive, I came to see how similar we are. As I look in the mirror today, I see my father when he was sixty-four, and as I reflect on my own idiosyncrasies — my impatience, my inclination to control things, and my style of talking — I quickly see that the main difference between us is age, not character! Few adult sons have the opportunity to come to know their fathers and spend time with them. It is a special grace that is given to me during this sabbatical. We like to be together. My father likes his place as the patriarch, he likes good hotels, good restaurants, and good art. He likes interesting conversation, good manners, preferential treatment, and excellent service. And he likes for me to pay the bills! Not because he has no money or is stingy but because he likes to have a son who can pay for his father.

My father is interested in me, but more in my health than in my work, more in my clothes than in my books, more in my German friends than in my American friends. He is a real European from the old school. A long time ago when we had a conflict, he said, "As a psychologist you know everything about authoritarian fathers. Try to be happy that you have one, but don't try to change him!"

Today I enjoy being with my father. The less I want to change him the more he enjoys being with me and sharing his vulnerability. As we both have become "elders," our needs have become quite similar. We both like solitude, quiet time, restful spaces, good friends, good food, and a peaceful atmosphere. Our common interests in art, literature, and the spiritual life give us a lot to talk about. When I was thirty-two and my father was sixty-one, we belonged to different generations and we were far apart. Today it seems that we have become part of the same generation and grown very close, close to death and close to each other. I thank God for my father. Whatever happens to him in the coming year, I will always be grateful that we had this unique time together.

Utrecht, Holland,
Sunday, January 7

It was a real surprise when a few days ago Rodleigh called. "Where are you?" I asked. "We are in Zwolle," he said, "and we have been trying to reach you ever since we came to Holland. Can you come to visit us?"

I was so excited to hear from my trapeze friends. The last time I saw them was a year ago. Now the question was how to make it to Zwolle before Sunday night, when the Flying Rodleighs would all leave for their vacations in South Africa and the United States. This morning was the only possibility. I called Jan and asked him whether he would like to come with me.

At 10:45 this morning Jan and I found each other at the train station in Zwolle, and ten minutes later we were sitting with Rodleigh and his wife, Jennie, in their caravan. Soon we also saw Jonathon, Karlene, Kailene, Slava, and John. It felt so good to see them all again. I realized how much I had missed being with them.

Rodleigh told us about the hard times they had recently lived through: complicated problems with their caravans, serious health problems, and most of all the death of Raedawn, Rodleigh and Karlene's sister, in Italy. After hearing about Raedawn's death, Rodleigh had bought a car and driven alone to Reggio, where the funeral and burial were to be. There Raedawn's friends had taken him to the morgue to see his sister. He didn't want to go, since he had never seen a dead person and wanted to remember his sister the way she was during her last visit, but they didn't let him break their traditions. Seeing his sister's emaciated body so shocked Rodleigh that he wept for two days. Listening to all of this, I was amazed

88

that the Flying Rodleighs hadn't canceled a single perform-ance. Recently Jennie stopped working in the act, but Kerri, a sixteen-year-old girl from South Africa, had been trained to take her place.

As always, Rodleigh explained things with great clarity and systematically, like a teacher. He wanted me to know every-thing and took his time recounting it, even though a few hours later the troupe would be on their way to Hannover to park their caravan there until March.

At 12:30 Rodleigh took Jan and me to the show. It was a very fine show, but few people came to see it. Uncharacteris-tically the Rodleighs performed poorly. Because of the hall's low ceiling, the whole act had been toned down, and the two most spectacular tricks failed. Both Slava and Rodleigh missed their catcher, John, and ended up in the net. The huge, largely empty building didn't offer a worthy context for these very artistic performers.

Between the Flying Rodleighs' act and the finale, Jan and I had tea with Karlene and Jonathon in their caravan. Since I last saw them, Karlene and Jonathon have fallen in love and become a couple. Kailene, Karlene's daughter, was happy to have a real family now. We had a good and lively visit.

Before the second show started, Rodleigh drove Jan and me to the station. As I reflected on this short visit, I realized how good it had been for me. I am looking forward to being with the Flying Rodleighs again in June or July . . . and to realizing my long-held dream to write a book about them. The desire to do this had even grown after I listened to Rodleigh and Jennie's negative response to the New Year's TV program. They felt that their act was poorly shown and poorly integrated into the whole of the program. Since I haven't seen the program yet I couldn't respond well, but I experienced a new impulse to write about the troupe in ways that they themselves could appreciate.

At 5:30 p.m. we arrived in Utrecht. Jan took me right away to Pays Bas, the hotel where he had made a reservation for me. I really liked my room there and decided to stay for a week.

Monday, January 8

I was invited for dinner and the Eucharist at the Ariens-convict, the formation center for future priests for the dioceses of Utrecht and Groningen. I was very glad to go there and connect with my own diocese in that way.

What a contrast with the time I was at the seminary! In those days there were hundreds of eager candidates. I lived in the same large building for six years. The discipline was strict, the lifestyle simple and solid, the teaching very traditional and conservative. I could only leave the building in the company of others. My great contribution to the "liberation" of the seminary was bicycles! I convinced the staff that having bikes was good for seminarians. Anyhow, those were the '50s, and the Second Vatican Council was still far away.

The Ariensconvict is a beautiful old-fashioned house in downtown Utrecht where theology students live with their rector while studying theology at the university. All together there are thirty-six students, and there is a concern that few new men are applying and that in the future fewer and fewer priests will be ordained.

During dinner I had an opportunity to introduce myself to the students. The atmosphere was quite friendly and relaxed. Although the institutional quality of the large seminary was gone and the atmosphere was more like a family, it was clearly a miniature seminary, and the discussions, interests, and preoccupations were similar to those of my time. The only woman was a sister who did the cooking.

The Eucharist was lovely but was a miniature of the old high church liturgy. It felt like an adaptation for a small group of a ceremony meant for large crowds. The celebrant, dressed in rich vestments, stood behind a stone altar in a cryptlike chapel. The students sat in a circle facing the altar. There were songs indicated on a board, readings from behind the lectern, a fine homily, and the seminarians received Holy Communion with much devotion. However, I doubt that a stranger would be able to guess that these people live together, eat together, and study together. The formality of the ritual appears to create distance in word, gesture, and movement that does not exist among these men immediately before or after the liturgy. In the celebration one seems to enter into a behavioral world that is separate from normal life. To see these men shaking hands with each other as a sign of peace when they had just finished dinner together was somewhat unreal to me, especially because nobody was leaving the building after the celebration! The homily seemed to be directed to strangers as opposed to those present who all live in the same house. That anyone would spontaneously speak or respond to the readings, or that there would be some kind of sharing seemed far-fetched in this context.

Tuesday, January 9

This morning I took the train to Haarlem to spend the day with my friend Jurjen. Jurjen is a capable, very intelligent, and deeply committed pastor who works in the inner city of Haarlem with the homeless, AIDS patients, and the poor, and who dedicates much of his time to writing and publishing about contemporary religious issues. His main focus is the integration of spirituality and social action in the pastoral work of the church. It is these themes that brought us together many years ago and continue to inspire us in our discussions: What is the place of prayer, contemplation, meditation, and the interior life in a ministry that responds to the immediate needs of the poor and oppressed? Can you be a monk as well as a social activist? Jurjen's history as a pastor in the Dutch Reformed Church has made him known as a significant social critic who calls the church to step out of its isolation and respond to "real problems." In this context a life of solitude, silence, and prayer easily looks "escapist."

Rotterdam, Holland, Sunday, January 14

... In the evening I finally had a chance to see the video of the TV program with the Flying Rodleighs. It was a lot better than I had expected. Less reflective than the English version and a little more fragmentary, but certainly lively and with many interesting connections between a life with handicapped people and a life with great athletes.

My main criticism is that footage of another trapeze act was used as if they were the Rodleighs. I could well understand Rodleigh being offended that his act was mixed up with that of another, unknown troupe. I could also understand Rodleigh's unhappiness that twice they showed a fall in the net, giving the impression of regular failure. But for outsiders all of this is quite secondary. The people who saw the program were enchanted. Laura, my niece with Down's syndrome, played her role beautifully. Her smile, her total absorption in the performance, and her spontaneity were delightful.

Prague, Czech Republic, Friday, January 19

This morning Jan and I took a KLM flight from Amsterdam to Prague. At the Prague Airport, Peter, a Dutch friend of

Jan who lives and teaches in Prague, was waiting for us. Peter will be our guide for the next three days. He speaks Czech fluently, knows Czech history from Wenceslas to Havel, has many contacts with Roman Catholic and Protestant groups, and is active in the Czech Pax Christi.

As we drove to the center of the city, Peter tried to answer my many questions about Jan Hus and the Hussites, about the violent struggles between Reformers and Counter-Reformers, about the influence of the Habsburgs, the Nazi domination, the Communist period, the final independence of Czechoslovakia in December 1989, and the split between the Czech Republic and Slovakia in 1993. In that short cab ride the names of the writers Max Brod, Franz Kafka, and Jaroslav Hašek, and the composers Bedřich Smetana and Antonín Dvořák were also mentioned. I realized that my head was full of little fragments of Czech history and culture. Peter helped me to put the pieces together and rediscover the mosaic.

After lunch in a very pleasant restaurant, Peter went home and Jan and I walked past the National Theatre, along the Moldau, and over the famous Charles Bridge, flanked by large Baroque statues of Christ and the saints. Walking over the bridge gave me the feeling of becoming part of a very painful period of history. The triumphalist Catholic statues erected in the seventeenth century speak of the victory of the Counter-Reformation over the reform movements that started with Jan Hus at the end of the fourteenth century. Talking to Peter later, I realized that even today the Catholic

Church is perceived by many of Prague's now-secularized citizens as a foreign, power-hungry institution. The hierarchy's desire to reclaim the St. Vitus Cathedral after the Communist domination is looked at by many with great suspicion.

Saturday, January 20

Since I have been in Prague I have learned a new word: *defenestration.* It means "throwing your opponent out the window." There is something of a tradition of defenestration in Prague. It happened on July 30, 1419, when the Hussites stormed the Town Hall and threw three consuls and seven citizens out the window, thus starting the Hussite wars. It happened again on the twenty-second of May 1618, when enraged citizens threw three councillors out the window of the Hradčany Castle into the moat (all of them survived because they landed in a dung heap). This confrontation led to the Thirty Years' War. It most likely happened again on the tenth of March 1948, when Jan Masaryk, the foreign minister of the Czech Republic, the only non-Communist cabinet member, was found dead in the courtyard. I had never heard of this strange "custom," but I have decided to keep my windows closed as long as I can here! . . .

Sunday, January 21

Before Jan and I came to Prague, Peter had spoken to Tomáš, the former secretary of the Czech bishops' conference and presently university chaplain, about our visit. Since three of my books, *The Genesee Diary*, *The Way of the Heart*, and *Life of the Beloved*, have been translated into Czech, he and several students knew about me. Tomáš invited me to concelebrate the 2:00 p.m. Eucharist in the San Salvador Church right across from the Charles Bridge and to give an afternoon conference for anyone who wanted to come.

The large Baroque church was extremely cold, and I wondered if anyone would come to Mass in such low temperatures. In the large sacristy, which was pleasantly heated, Tomáš greeted us. He impressed me as a strong personality — open, direct, and clearly progressive in church matters. He seemed to feel quite at ease with his role and gave me a few instructions about my place in the liturgy.

When we entered in a long procession with acolytes carrying the cross, candles, and the book, the church was packed with students, visitors, and friends. Many people had to remain standing during the service. It was so cold that I wondered if we would make it through the hour-long service. Happily, just before the procession the sacristan offered me a fur vest to wear under the alb. Without it I probably would not have been very attentive to the liturgy.

The Eucharist was simple. Everything happened reverently and traditionally. There was no difference between a Sunday Mass in Richmond Hill and this Sunday Mass in Prague, except for the language. Before the final blessing I introduced myself with a few words about my life at L'Arche Daybreak.

After the Eucharist about eighty people gathered in the large sacristy for the talk. The discussion afterward was quite lively. People were very gentle, kind, open, and attentive. They gave me great authority and hardly criticized my ideas. In contrast to my homeland, where most of what I say or write is subjected to critical scrutiny and is seldom accepted at face value, here everybody received my words more as support for their spiritual life than as something to be discussed. There was a certain obedient passivity in the audience but also a loving receptivity.

Afterward, one of Peter's friends said, "Some students felt you were too American — too much walking around, gesturing, and dramatic expression. We are not used to that here. We are more quiet and sedate." It is interesting for me, a Dutch man living in Canada, to be considered "too American." They should have said, "You were too Henri Nouwen!" They are right: I tend to exaggerate with my voice and overdramatize things, always afraid of boring people. But notwithstanding the criticism, I had the sense that most people found the meeting inspiring and uplifting.

Utrecht, Monday, January 22

Kathy called to tell me that Tim died last Saturday at 3:00 p.m. Although I was prepared for the news I felt much inner sorrow. A beautiful man of God has left us — his wife, his three little children, and his many close friends. I spoke to Phyllis by phone and later to his best friend's wife. There was so much pain and sadness. I sat down at my hotel desk and wrote a letter to Tim's family and friends explaining how he had deepened and strengthened my faith. What a grace to have known him. I wish I could go to the funeral, but I will feel very close to all who mourn Tim's death.

Wednesday, January 24

My sixty-fourth birthday. I am really glad to celebrate this day with my father. He felt well again and even took the car to go to the bank. Later we went to a friend's home to see the Rodleighs video. My father loved it. Meanwhile the heating system failed, so we had to keep ourselves warm with the open fire. Two old men sitting close to the fireplace warming their hands.

I feel happy on this day. Grateful to God and my family and friends for all the graces that have come to me during these sixty-four years. I look forward to the years to come as time to deepen my life with God and my friendship with people. I especially hope that I will have more space and time to write. Deep within myself I feel that something new wants to be born: a book with stories, a novel, a spiritual journal — something quite different from what I have done in the past. There is a sense of conclusion and new beginnings. This sabbatical year seems to be the year of transition from an active traveling life to a life of contemplation and writing. I realize, though, that it will require a lot of discipline to refocus my life. But without such a refocusing I will end up busy, restless, and always looking for human affirmation. It's time to make a radical choice for solitude, prayer, and quiet writing. I will need a lot of support to make this happen.

At 6:00 p.m. my father and I had dinner together in a nearby restaurant. We were the only guests! It was a delicious dinner, and we both enjoyed the quiet time together and all the attention we got from the waiter, who had only us to worry about!

This was probably the most quiet birthday of my life. But I will always remember it as the most peaceful.

Rotterdam, Saturday, January 27

A very special day! My sister, Laurien, organized a birthday party for me at her home in Nijmegen. She had invited several Dutch friends whom I had come to know at different stages of my life, but most of whom I had not seen for several years or even decades.

It was a unique evening for me, especially since everyone was in a very good mood and was eager to meet everyone else. Obviously the main question was, "What has happened with you since we last saw each other?" A lot had happened: most of all children and grandchildren. And jobs: Ferry a computer expert, Toon a businessman, Arnold a doctor, Louis a director of a TV and radio station, Wim a professor of child psychology, Jurjen a minister. Although all in the party were younger than I am, three of them — Ferry, Toon, and Henri — had already retired, and one of them, Louis, is going to say good-bye to his work at the end of next month.

What surprised me was that my friends were still in their first marriages and had also maintained some relationship with the church.

Obviously there were many "do you remember" stories. Most interesting for me was that each had stories to tell about me that I absolutely could not remember. Events that some of my friends remember with great vividness seem to have completely dropped out of my mind. And I carried ideas and images of my friends that were quite different from theirs.

The memories that we all most had in common were of our travels. Our bike trip to Belgium, our car trip to Germany, our boat trip to the island Spetsai in Greece, our plane trip to Israel, and all the events connected with these adventures....

Watertown, Wednesday, January 31

My brother Paul took me to the airport at 7:00 a.m., "before the traffic gets heavy," he said. We arrived at Schiphol at 8:00 a.m.

◆ ◆ ◆

Jonas welcomed me in Boston at 1:30 local time and drove me to my home away from home in Watertown. It is good to be back with Jonas, Margaret, and Sam.

Although I had been able to sleep a little on the plane, I was so tired that I went right to bed.

February 1996

Thursday, February 1

Many letters and many birthday gifts to open. Many phone calls to make and many little things to arrange for the move to New Jersey on Sunday.

The special event of today was Borys's visit. Since we last saw each other, Borys has been in Ukraine, Italy, California, and many places in between. Just as I returned from Holland he returned from a month-long retreat with the monks of the Ukrainian Monastery in California.

It was very good to be together again. Our friendship becomes deeper and stronger as the years pass. Borys, who often looks exhausted and overworked, now looks rested and relaxed. It became clear to both of us how important we are for each other. "One day we should travel together," Borys said. I could hear his desire for a companion on his many journeys, someone to pray with, to talk with, and just to be with. I felt quite grateful to be and become more and more a true spiritual partner with him.

The retreat had given Borys a new focus, a new perspective, and a new energy. "Somehow I nearly lost God in my busy life for God," he said. "I am so glad to have refound my first love." I often wonder where we both will be ten, twenty, or thirty years from today. I hope and pray we will still be together and close to God.

Friday, February 2

The Feast of the Presentation of Jesus in the Temple. Borys, Jonas, and I celebrated the Eucharist together in the Empty Bell. Very quiet, very peaceful, very serene. Jonas played the shakuhachi to put us in a spirit of prayer and focus our minds and hearts on God. We read the moving story of old Simeon, who recognized the child Jesus as the light coming into the darkness, and we shared the bread and cup as signs of God's presence among us. . . .

Tonight Borys will be here again. I look forward to a restful evening.

Saturday, February 3

At 11:30 a.m. Jutta came for a farewell visit. We had a lovely lunch at a nearby diner. Hamburgers! As always Jutta came with many gifts. Tulips, chocolates, coffee, and a book of essays about May Sarton. I am deeply grateful for Jutta's faithfulness to me even when I am such a poor friend.

This was such a hard week for her in the nursing home. Two people to whom she was very close died. She gave them and their families all her attention. But who is there for her when she comes home at night? Who cares for her in the way she cares for others? Her loneliness is deep and painful. She knows it and she accepts it, but it is a great cross to bear.

Peapack, Sunday, February 4

After the Eucharist in the Empty Bell, Jonas and I drove to Peggy's home in Peapack, where I will stay for the second part of my sabbatical. We had a joyful trip, and I am so grateful for Jonas's willingness to go with me. It was very cold but sunny. The roads were clear even though the meadows and hills were all still covered with snow.

It took us less than five hours to make it to Peggy's home. Dorothy, Peggy's housekeeper, welcomed us kindly and showed us the little house that will be my place for the coming months. It is quite spacious: a living room with kitchen and two bedrooms. Jonas took a walk while I tried to find places to put my things. I am really glad to have a new home and a quiet place to write. January was a good month, especially the time with my father, but it will be good to be in the same place for a little longer and to sit at a table again, working with ideas and the words to express them.

Monday, February 5

After we celebrated the Eucharist together I took Jonas to Bernardsville, where he caught the bus to New York. He will visit Crossroad, which is publishing his "Rebecca" book, before returning to Boston.

Tuesday, February 6

My Boston editor, Susan, gave me a copy of an excerpt from Mark Epstein's book *Thoughts without a Thinker: Psychotherapy from a Buddhist Perspective*. I found it a true eye-opener.

Epstein writes about the first cross-cultural meeting of Eastern masters and Western therapists, where the Dalai Lama was incredulous at the pervasiveness of "low self-esteem" that he kept hearing about. It seems that in the Tibetan cosmology, such feelings represent "the hungry ghost realm," not the human realm. In Tibet one assumes a positive sense of self, which is inculcated early and supported through all of the interdependent relationships that are established by the web of family. So a person is expected to maintain this positive feeling about himself, and if he cannot, he is considered a fool.

I find the concept of "hungry ghosts" fascinating. Epstein's theory is that Western feelings of unworthiness are rooted in the "hungry ghost" scenario because we are prematurely estranged in our childhoods. Thus, many of us are unable to find or sustain intimacy in our adult lives so we become preoccupied instead with the unresolved frustrations of our past. Indeed, it seems that many of us hope to find a solution to our low self-esteem by exploring our past, but in doing so we often drown in the many complicated waves of our personal histories. It is the hungry ghost, looking for a satisfaction that cannot be found.

The hungry ghosts, Epstein says, "are probably the most vividly drawn metaphors in the [Buddhist] Wheel of Life." He describes them as "phantomlike creatures with withered limbs, grossly bloated bellies, and long, narrow necks." In addition, the ghosts, when they eat or drink to satisfy their hunger, suffer from terrible pain and indigestion. Their throats burn, their bellies are unable to digest food, and they cannot take transitory satisfaction. So they remain obsessed with a fantasy of finding complete freedom from pain, especially the pain of the past, but they are ignorant of the fact that this desire is a fantasy.

When Jesus appears to his disciples after his resurrection, they think they are seeing a ghost. But Jesus says, "Why are you so agitated, and why are these doubts stirring in your hearts? See by my hands and my feet that it is I myself. Touch me and see for yourselves; a ghost has no flesh and bones as you can see I have" (Lk 24:38–39).

The Buddhist vision of hungry ghosts and the Christian vision of the resurrection supplement each other. By claiming our presence here and now, and by acknowledging our unfulfilled needs without wanting to fill them up with "food" from the past, we too can come to the joy the disciples experienced when they saw the risen Lord, who took grilled fish and ate it before their eyes (see Lk 24:43).

I am increasingly convinced that it is possible to live the wounds of the past not as gaping abysses that cannot be filled and therefore keep threatening us but as gateways to new life. The "gateless gate" of Zen and the "healing wounds of Christ" both encourage us to detach ourselves from the past and trust in the *glory* to which we are called.

Wednesday, February 7

It seems that I evoked the hungry ghost in me while writing about it! This whole day I felt like a hungry ghost: hungry for attention and affection — telephone calls, letters, and so on. I ended up angry, not only at all those who didn't give me what I craved but also at my own hungry spirit for being so needy. I know that, after all the traveling and moving around of the last two months, it is time for silence, prayer, quiet writing, and just being alone. But my hungry ghost kept me restless, looking for little distractions, and thus avoiding a direct confrontation, which would make that ghost stop complaining so much.

After spending some time in the nearby town of Chester and buying a few things I really don't need, I sat down in front of the galleys of my cup book, which was a setup for frustration! All the way through I knew that the problem was not the book; it was my hungry ghost, feeling abandoned, rejected, forgotten.

Happily I found some consolation in my evening prayers. Somehow, saying them out loud, nearly screaming in the empty house, I started to experience little bits of inner peace.

Thursday, February 8

A difficult day again. I feel lonely, depressed, and unmotivated. Most of the day I have been fiddling around with little things. The same old pain that has been with me for many years and never seems to go completely away.

Meanwhile I have been playing with a new fax machine, which arrived yesterday. I was able to put the pieces together by following the instructions in the booklet, and to my great surprise it worked! I drove to Flanders, a little town ten miles from Peapack, to find a stationery store and buy the right kind of paper for it.

I realize that my busyness is a way to keep my depression at bay. It doesn't work. I have to pray more. I know that I need to just sit in God's presence and show God all my darkness. But everything in me rebels against that. Still, I know it is the only way out.

A few very kind letters gave me a little light.

God help me, be with me, console me, and take the cloud away from my heart.

Saturday, February 10

At 9:00 a.m., Peggy, Phil, and I celebrated the Eucharist together in the second bedroom of the guesthouse where I am staying. It was a beautiful, intimate prayer time.

Richmond Hill, Ontario, Monday, February 12

This morning after the Eucharist, Kathy called from Toronto to tell me that Adam Arnett had had a severe setback — a possible heart attack combined with an epileptic seizure — and had been rushed to the hospital. Shortly afterward I talked to Nathan, and I realized that Adam was dying. I wanted to fly home immediately, and Nathan encouraged me to do so.

Adam is one of the men who introduced me into the community of L'Arche Daybreak and led me into a whole spirituality of weakness that has transformed my life. Living together with Adam at L'Arche Daybreak has profoundly influenced my prayer, my sense of myself, my spirituality, and my ministry. Adam, the man who suffers from severe epilepsy, and whose life has seemingly been limited because of his many disabilities, has touched the lives of hundreds of L'Arche assistants, visitors, and friends. As my friend and housemate he has reached into the depths of my heart and has touched my life beyond words.

Arriving in Toronto I was held up in immigration since I had been out of the country for so long. But finally I made it through all the checkpoints. Nathan was waiting for me and told me what he knew about Adam's situation. We drove directly to the hospital.

Rex and Jeanne, Adam's parents, greeted me, and we were happy to see each other. Several members of the Daybreak community were there to support Rex and Jeanne and to stay close to Adam in these last hours of his life.

When I walked into Adam's room, he was breathing rather regularly with the help of an oxygen mask. Ann, the person responsible for Adam's home, said, "This morning, shortly after he was brought to the hospital, Adam's heart stopped, and the doctor declared that he had died. But after several minutes his heartbeat and breathing returned. It seemed he was not yet ready to die. I'm sure he was waiting for Rex, Jeanne, and you."

I was deeply moved to see my friend Adam lying there, obviously living his final hours with us. I kissed him on the forehead and stroked his hair.

After half an hour just looking at Adam and talking quietly with Rex and Jeanne, I invited all those in the waiting room to gather around Adam's bed. We held hands and prayed for Adam, for his parents and family, and for his many friends. After that we just sat with him, following his breathing.

An hour later Michael, Adam's brother, came. It was clear that Michael was suffering immensely, and when he saw his brother he began to cry. His father embraced him. A few minutes later, when he saw me, he threw his arms around me and cried. I held his shaking body for a long time and then went with him again to Adam's bed.

Michael is also a member of Daybreak and, like Adam, suffers from epilepsy. I asked Michael to hold the little container with sacred oil, and, while everyone gathered again,

I anointed Adam's forehead and both of his hands, praying fervently that God would give him the strength to make the passage to his final home in peace.

"My, my, my... brother... is going... to heaven," Michael said through his tears. "My heart is broken. My heart is broken, Father." I held him again, and we cried together.

Around 6:00 p.m. Nathan and I went to the Church Street House to fetch the food that the assistants had prepared for Jeanne and Rex, and then we had a quiet supper at a nearby restaurant.

When we returned to the hospital, Adam was in a different room because he no longer needed the heart monitors. Adam was now close to death, and the only thing to do was to make him as comfortable as possible. He was still wearing a face mask to help his breathing, but it seemed to make little difference. Finally Rex and Ann removed the mask so that Adam could be free from all unnecessary support systems. His breathing was slow and deep; once in a while it stopped but then started again. Now he was clearly struggling. Although it seemed that he was not having any pain, it was painful to see Adam fighting for every breath. Jeanne said, "With a weak heart like his, I can't understand how he can do it... it is such a struggle." Rex knelt beside the bed and held Adam's hand; Jeanne stood on the other side with her hands on his knees. I sat at the top of the bed caressing his head and hair, and once in a while holding his face between my hands.

The hours went by, and by midnight it seemed that Adam would make it through the night. Nathan and others from Daybreak had gone home, and I started to feel my own exhaustion. Ann said, "Go home now and get some sleep. Rex, Jeanne, and I will be here, and we will call you when Adam dies."

Just after I had fallen asleep at the Dayspring, Ann called and said, "Henri, Adam has died." Adam's life — and mission — had come to its end. I thought of Jesus' words "It is fulfilled." Fifteen minutes later I was back at the hospital. Adam lay there, completely still, at peace. Rex and Jeanne and Ann were sitting beside the bed touching Adam's body. There were tears, tears of grief but also of gratitude. We held hands, and, while touching Adam's body, we prayed in thanksgiving for the thirty-four years of his life and for all that he had brought to us in his great physical weakness and incredible spiritual strength.

I couldn't keep my eyes away from him. I thought, here is the man who more than anyone has connected me with God and the Daybreak community. Here is the man whom I cared for during my first year at Daybreak and have come to love so much. Here is the one I have written about, talked about all over Canada and the United States. Here is my counselor, teacher, and guide, who never could say a word to me but taught me more than anyone else. Here is Adam, my friend, my beloved friend, the most vulnerable of all the people I have ever known and at the same time the most

111

powerful. He is dead now. His life is over. His face is still. I felt immense sadness and immense gratitude. I have lost a companion but gained a guardian for the rest of my life. May all the angels guide him into paradise and welcome him home to the embrace of his loving God.

As I looked at Adam, I saw how beautiful he was. Here was a young man at peace. A long, long suffering had come to an end. His beautiful spirit was no longer imprisoned in a body that could not help to express it. I asked myself about the deepest meaning of these thirty-four years of captivity. But that will only gradually be revealed. Now we simply have to trust and to rest.

Tuesday, February 13

At 8:30 a.m. we celebrated the Eucharist in the Dayspring chapel. Before that I had gone to the Red House to tell Michael and all his housemates that Adam had died. I also went to Adam's house to be for a moment with his housemates, and to the Green House to talk to the people there, especially Bill and David, who had been very close to Adam. There were many tears and long embraces. We so need one another at moments like these.

During the Eucharist Michael was sitting on my right. He had put on his alb and kept holding my hand. Gordie and Francis had also vested themselves to be altar servants. I chose to speak about the resurrection of Lazarus. Somehow our faith in the resurrection of the body is very important at this time. Adam's body, which we all had touched and held so often in his long struggle for survival, will be renewed. In the resurrection he will be dressed with a body that will allow him to express the deepest stirrings of his heart. We are full of tears as Mary, Martha, and Jesus were at the death of their brother and friend, but it is not the end. It is the passage to glory, to victory, to freedom. I could see how we all experienced enormous sadness because of Adam's leaving but also an immense joy that he was finally free.

At the end of mass, Gordie got up and addressed Michael directly: "I know your heart is broken, Michael, but I'd like you to have this." Then he hung a Special Olympics medal, which was dear to him, around Michael's neck. Michael was visibly moved by Gordie's kindness.

◆ ◆ ◆

Being back at Daybreak means seeing many friends again. Kathy and Timmy, Carl, Kathy and Margaret, Joe and Stephanie, and many others. Sue is away but will return tomorrow.

...At 6:00 p.m. Joe, Carl, Nathan, and I had dinner. I was fighting fatigue since I had hardly slept last night and was wondering how to stay awake and alert through our meeting. But somehow being with good and caring friends energized me and made the tiredness move to the background of my consciousness.

Wednesday, February 14

Today at 2:00 p.m. I went to the funeral home in Richmond Hill. Seeing Adam's body in his casket touched me deeply. He looked so peaceful, like a young man who had just fallen asleep. Tears filled my eyes. Our relationship has had such a deep impact on my life journey. I looked at his beautiful and gentle face, and I felt profoundly humble and grateful to have been in his circle of friends. I couldn't stop looking at him. He looked so normal, so healthy, and so handsome. It was as if he was giving me a glimpse of the new body he would have in the resurrection. . . .

Within an hour the room where Adam's body was laid out was full of people from the community, family, and friends. I was touched to recognize that Greg who had lived with Adam for a few years, had come with his wife Eileen, from Chicago, that Steve who had grown close to Adam when he was an assistant at the Day Programme, flew in from Seattle, and Peter who had accompanied Adam for two years in his home, had traveled from Nova Scotia to be with us all at this time. At 3:00 p.m. we formed a large circle and prayed. Then I asked whether anyone wanted to tell a story about Adam, and various people spoke of special moments in their relationships with Adam. Rex's and others' "little stories" brought smiles and laughter, and made us aware of how, beyond all words, all memories and images, this simple, poor man had shown us the gentle face of God.

When at 7:00 p.m. many of us gathered to be with Adam for two more hours, the mood was different: more relaxed, more festive, more playful. As we formed another circle, Kathy and Elizabeth, two community members, told moving stories, not about what they had experienced with Adam but about how they would see him again. Everybody listening felt the joy and peace that came from their words. Here we were, standing around Adam's body, imagining his newfound freedom and celebrating his newfound life. Then we sang "Peace Is Flowing Like a River."

Adam, the peacemaker, is finally free from all captivity. In his brokenness he has shown me my own brokenness, and thus set me on the road to healing and new life. Now he will receive a new body, full of light, full of love, full of glory, the reward of his remarkable mission.

Thursday, February 15

By 9:00 a.m. I was in St. Mary's Immaculate Catholic Church with my suitcases full of chalices, patens, and colorful altar cloths, plus my homily notes written out in my journal book. By 9:45 several hundred people from all over had gathered to celebrate the life and death of Adam Arnett.

As eight of Adam's close friends accompanied the casket to the front of the church, we all sang "The Beatitudes," and during the service we listened to the words of St. Paul, "God chose those who by human standards are weak to shame the strong" (1 Cor. 1:27).

Adam didn't need a eulogy. His simple, hidden life had no impressive curriculum vitae. But Adam deserved to be praised for the miracles he had worked in our hearts. His father, Rex, Ann, his long-time friend and head of his home, and Bill, one of his housemates, spoke about these miracles in a simple and moving way. All three of them told stories about how Adam had reached a deep place in them that few people had been able to reach and he had planted there little seeds of hope.

As I have lived these last three days, I've come to see with a clarity I never had before that Adam was the living Christ among us. Where else did we have to go to be with the man of sorrow and the man of joy? Where else did we have to look for the presence of God? Yes, Adam was loved by God long before his parents, his brother, or we, loved him. Yes, Adam was sent by God to live among us, a hard but blessed life for thirty-four years. And yes, Adam, after completing his mission, was called back home to God to live a new life in a new body. That's the story of Jesus. That's the story of Adam too!

I know, too, that L'Arche became my community and Daybreak my home because of Adam — because of holding Adam in my arms and touching him in complete purity and complete freedom. He called me home. It was not just a home with good people, but it was a home in my own body, in the body of my community, in the body of the church, yes, in the body of God. Without him I do not know where I would be today.

As I was holding the bread in my hands, standing in front of Adam's body, and speaking Jesus' words "Take and eat, this is my Body given for you," I saw, in a whole new way, the mystery of God, of Adam, and of each one of us. Indeed in Christ, God had taken a body so that we could touch God and be healed. I sensed today that God's body and Adam's body are one, because, as Jesus says, "In so far as you did this to one of the least of my brethren you did it to me" (Mt 25:40). In Adam, indeed, we touched the living Christ among us. And, as with Jesus, everyone who touched Adam was healed.

◆ ◆ ◆

At the cemetery the pallbearers carried Adam's body to the burial site and placed it on the metal structure above the grave.

After a short prayer, I gave Michael the holy-water sprinkler, and, while I held him tightly, he bent over his brother's casket and carefully blessed it, slowly walking from one side to the other. Then I prayed: "Dear God, into your hands we commend our son, brother, and friend Adam. Welcome Adam to paradise, and help us to comfort each other."

Adam's casket was lowered into the grave, and I was hit by the finality of his death. He was gone and would never be with us again. St. Paul says it with so much conviction: "What is sown is perishable, but what is raised is imperishable; what is sown is contemptible but what is raised is glorious; what is sown is weak, but what is raised is powerful; what is sown is a natural body, and what is raised is a spiritual body" (1 Cor 15:42–44). It was right in front of that big hole that I was confronted with the finality of death as well as with the hope in the resurrection. . . .

Peapack, Saturday, February 17

Jay took me to the Port Authority bus station, where I caught the 10:00 a.m. bus to Bernardsville. Peggy was there to take me home. . . .

Monday, February 19

Today's Gospel is about the cure of a boy possessed by a demon who makes him dumb and throws him constantly into fire and water.

Two aspects of healing are clear here. First of all, we have to trust in the healer. Jesus says, "All things can be done for the one who believes" (Mk 9:24). Second, the healer must be a person of prayer. When the disciples ask Jesus, "Why could we not cast it out?" Jesus says, "This kind can come out only through prayer and fasting" (Mk 9:29).

I am touched by this mutuality between the healer and the person who needs healing. Healers must be in communion with the source of all life and healing so that they can be true mediators of the healing power, which is larger than themselves. People who seek healing must surrender themselves, trusting that the healer can indeed mediate that healing power to them. The humility of the healer and the faith of the sick person are both central to the work of healing.

Tuesday, February 20

Most of the day I spent writing about Adam's death and funeral. Although my emotional and spiritual fatigue is still with me, I am able to write a bit, and to use my writing as a way of grieving.

Ash Wednesday, February 21

I am certainly not ready for Lent yet. Christmas seems just behind us, and Lent seems an unwelcome guest. I could have used a few more weeks to get ready for this season of repentance, prayer, and preparation for the death and resurrection of Jesus. But this morning quite a few gathered for the Eucharist. Peggy had brought some ashes, and I put on my alb and Guatemalan stole to mark the special quality of the day.

I spoke about how Jesus stressed the hidden life. Whether we give alms, pray, or fast, we are to do it in a hidden way, not to be praised by people but to enter into closer communion with God. Lent is a time of returning to God. It is a time to confess how we keep looking for joy, peace, and satisfaction in the many people and things surrounding us, without really finding what we desire. Only God can give us what we want. So we must be reconciled with God, as Paul says, and let that reconciliation be the basis of our relationships with others.

Lent is a time of refocusing, of reentering the place of truth, of reclaiming our true identity.

After the reflections on the Gospel, we put ashes on one another's foreheads. Later when I came to the post office, I saw Eugene, the postmaster of Peapack, with a big black mark on his forehead. For a moment I had forgotten all about ashes and thought he had hurt himself, but then I realized that he and I had the same mark, and we laughed together seeing it!

Thursday, February 22

When you can say to Jesus, "You are the Messiah, the Son of the living God," Jesus can say to you, "You are the rock on whom I will build my church." There is a mutuality of recognition and a mutuality of truth here. When we acknowledge that God has come among us through the Messiah — his anointed one — to free us from our captivity, God can point to our solid core and make us the foundation for a community of faith.

Our "rock" quality will be revealed to us when we confess our need for salvation and healing. We can become community builders when we are humble enough to see our dependence on God.

It is sad that the dialogue between Jesus and Simon Peter has, in my church, been almost exclusively used to explain the role of the papacy. By doing so, it seems to me that we miss seeing that this exchange is for all of us. We all have to confess our need for salvation, and we all have to accept our solid center.

And the keys of the Kingdom? They too belong first to all who confess Jesus as their Christ and thus come to belong to a community of faith in which our binding and unbinding happen in the Name of God. When indeed the body of Christ, formed by believers, makes decisions about its members, these are Kingdom decisions. That is what Jesus refers to when he says, "Whatever you bind on earth will be bound in heaven, and whatever you loose on earth will be loosed in heaven" (Mt 16:19).

These thoughts came to my mind on this Feast of the Chair of St. Peter, as we were gathering around the table with several people who had left the Catholic Church because they saw it as too authoritarian. More than ever it is important to realize that the Church is not simply "over there," where the bishops are or where the Pope is, but "right here," where we are around the table of the Lord.

New York, Friday, February 23

Today is Wendy's birthday. I took the bus from Bernardsville to New York to be with Wendy and Jay, and their son, Jonathan. Wendy had asked me to celebrate the Eucharist at 6:30 p.m. for the small circle of friends she had invited for dinner. Many of them belong to her prayer group. I met some remarkable people.

As we reflected on the readings and expressed our need for God's healing grace, it became clear how much suffering there was in the little group — depression, loss of family members through an accident and through AIDS, conflict with authorities, a close relative with a mental handicap, and the great stresses of New York City life. I spoke a little about the ways absence and presence touch each other. Precisely where we feel most present to each other we experience deeply the absence of those we love. And precisely at moments of great loss we can discover a new sense of closeness and intimacy. This is also what the Eucharist is about. We announce the presence of Christ among us until he comes again! There is both presence *and* absence, closeness *and* distance, an experience of at-homeness on the way home.

I was struck again by the paradox that loving someone deeply means opening yourself to the pain of her or his absence. Lent is a time to get in touch with our experience of absence, emptiness, unfulfillment, so that in the midst of our overcrowded lives we can remind ourselves that we are still waiting for the One who has promised to fulfill our deepest desires.

Sunday, February 25

The Eucharist this morning brought quite a few people together. The Genesis reading about the creation and fall of

Adam and Eve and the Gospel reading about the temptation of Christ spoke to me in a new way.

Adam and Eve were tempted to be like God. Jesus was tempted to deny his divine Sonship. When we act as if we are God, we cause war, but when we act as God's beloved children, we create peace. When we acknowledge God as our creator and Lord, we open ourselves to the news of Jesus that indeed we are God's children, eternally beloved, destined for a life eternal.

What especially struck me were the serpent's words "Your eyes will be opened, and you will be like God." When Adam and Eve do eat from the tree the storyteller says, "Then the eyes of both were opened, and they knew that they were naked" (Gen 3:5–7). But Jesus came to open our eyes to the deeper truth that, even though we are sinners, we are still God's beloved children. "Blessed are your eyes because they see," he says (Mt 13:16).

Both temptation stories are about our true spiritual identity.

Monday, February 26

Today's readings complement each other in a remarkable way. In the first reading, Moses says, "You shall not steal; . . . you shall not defraud. . . . You shall not revile the deaf. You shall not render an unjust judgment. . . . You shall not hate in your heart," and so on (Lv 19:11–17). The *nots* sound harsh and forbidding, like gunshots. But in the second reading, Jesus

says, "I was hungry and you gave me food, I was thirsty
and you gave me something to drink, I was a stranger and
you welcomed me.... Just as you did it to one of the least
of these brothers and sisters of mine, you did it to me"
(Mt 25:35, 40).

This is the great movement from "you shall not" to "you
may." We may care for the poor, the sick, and the dying, and
meet God there. Instead of a distant God, whom we must
please by not doing evil things, Jesus reveals to us a God who
is as close to us as the poorest person is.

I keep marveling at the radicality as well as the simplicity
of Jesus' message. He breaks right through all the questions
about what to do in order not to offend God and places the
poor in front of us, saying, "This is me...love me." How
radical and how simple!

Wednesday, February 28

"This evil generation...asks for a sign," Jesus says in today's
Gospel (Lk 11:29). But what we are looking for is right under
our eyes. Somehow we don't fully trust that our God is a God
of the present and speaks to us where we are. "This is the
day the Lord has made." When the people of Nineveh heard
Jonah speak, they turned back to God. Can we listen to the
word that God speaks to us today and do the same? This is a
very simple but crucial message: Don't wait for tomorrow to
change your heart. This is the favorable time!...

En route to Santa Fe, New Mexico, Thursday, February 29

Last year when I was planning my sabbatical, Malcolm, a dear friend from Texas, said to me, "If you ever want to spend some time in my house in Santa Fe, just let me know." It felt like a wonderful idea. Although I have been in Santa Fe a few times on my way to the Benedictine Monastery of Christ in the Desert in Abiquiu, and once to preach at the ordination and installation of my friend, Wayne, as a pastor there, I really hardly know the city or the state. But everyone who knows Santa Fe has told me, "Go, you will enjoy it. It is one of the loveliest places in the United States."

I took Malcolm up on his invitation. He suggested March first through tenth as the best time, and here I am, flying to New Mexico. Malcolm will meet me at Albuquerque Airport and drive me to Santa Fe. He and his daughter Alison will get me settled in their house and leave me there on Saturday. But I won't be alone. My longtime friend Frank, a Presbyterian minister from California, will join me on Saturday and we will spend the week together. I am excited, full of expectation, and open to new things.

March 1996

Santa Fe, Friday, March 1

Last night Alison and Malcolm were waiting for me at the Albuquerque Airport. It was good to see them again. Around 11:30 p.m. local time we made it to his house in Santa Fe. A small, intimate, romantic adobe condominium. An ideal place to spend a week....

Monday, March 4

At noon Frank and I visited Jim, who is the president of a small publishing house in Santa Fe. Jim is a longtime friend of my friend Fred, who had said to me, "When you go to Santa Fe, be sure to visit my friend Jim." It was a delightful visit. During lunch we spoke about our personal histories, spirituality, books, and of course, Santa Fe.

I was deeply touched by Jim's kindness, openness, honesty, and intelligence. He loves his work, is very committed to his role as editor and publisher, has a great interest in spiritual subjects, and radiates humility as well as self-confidence. One remark he made shows his personality. He said, "I love to help people, but I get very embarrassed when they thank me."

Wednesday, March 6

Tonight at 6:00 Jim came for dinner. Frank and I had so much enjoyed our time with him last Monday that we invited him to spend the evening with us.

After dinner I showed Jim the video *Angels over the Net* about the Flying Rodleighs and told him that I wanted to write a book about them but still hadn't found the right form. It has been five years since I met the Rodleighs. I have collected many notebooks of information about their lives, their art, and their ideas, but whenever I start to write I experience an enormous hesitation, even fear.

Jim responded quite radically: "You must write the book because you have given it so much of your energy and attention. You have to trust your intuition that your friendship with these trapeze artists allows you to say something very important."

I said, "Yes, that intuition is strong, but I am afraid. When I first saw the Rodleighs, something very deep and intimate within me was touched. They brought back in a vivid way the longings I had had as a seventeen-year-old boy for communion, community, and intimacy. Many of these longings went underground during my time at the seminary and the university and my years of teaching. They only manifested themselves in occasional mental wanderings, curiosities, and feelings of anguish. When I went to L'Arche I allowed all these feelings and emotions and passions to reemerge. But seeing the Rodleighs catapulted me into a new consciousness. There in the air I saw the artistic realization of my deepest yearnings. It was so intense that even today I do not dare to write about it because it requires a radical new step not only in my writing but also in my life."

Jim said, "I knew all this. The video showed it to me. The Rodleighs are completing something within you that for many years remained uncompleted. It has to do with your search for community and your deep yearning for completeness. If you do not write the book you will deny yourself an enormous opportunity for growth. Yes, it feels risky, and it is difficult, but you really have no choice."

I said, "But what is the book finally about?"

He answered, "About community, in the most universal sense. Through the Rodleighs' story you can express the longing of all people. It is not just about flying and catching but about that invisible community that undergirds all you are seeing in the Rodleighs. You see friendship, family, cooperation, artistic expression, love, commitment, and much more. It all has to do with community. And that's your final subject. It is like DOS in the computer world: the invisible force that keeps everything together. It is a metaphysical principle that holds the stars, the sun, and the moon in their orbits, that connects God with humanity, that allows people to fall in love and bring forth new life. It is the mysterious, ungraspable, and inexpressible reality on which everything else is based. It is that reality that you must touch through the image of the trapeze. Your life now is already very much involved in all of this. You cannot ignore it for much longer. You have to express it. For you that means writing about it...."

Sunday, March 10

We were back at the house in the early evening. After a light meal and evening prayers we went to bed early, planning to leave at 5:00 a.m. tomorrow to be on time for our flights to San Francisco and Newark.

Tuesday, March 12

The days in Santa Fe, simple and unpretentious as they were, revealed to me in a new way the beauty of life. Friendship, art, nature, history, and the tangible presence of the immanent as well as transcendent love of God filled me with gratitude for being alive and being alive with others.

In Santa Fe both agony and ecstasy are imprinted on the buildings and monuments and reflected in the many adobe houses. I well understand why painters, sculptors, writers, and musicians like to live there. Many great people have left their spirits in Santa Fe to protect as well as inspire them. During this short stay I experienced the presence of these spirits and got a glimpse of the permanent reality shining through the impermanence of all created things. Malcolm, Alison, Jim, Wayne, and most of all Frank became the ones who helped me to keep the heavy curtains of life's theater slightly open and encouraged me with their love and affection to trust that there is a great show being prepared for us.

Thursday, March 14

Jesus says, "Whoever is not with me is against me, and whoever does not gather with me scatters" (Lk 11:23). These words frighten me. I want to be with Jesus, but often it feels like I want to be with many others too! There is within me a strong tendency to play it safe. I want to stay friends with everyone. I do not like conflict or controversy. I hate divisions and confrontations among people. Is this a weakness, a lack of courage to speak out forcefully, a fear of rejection, a preoccupation with being liked? Or is it a strength that allows me to bring people together and be reconciled, to create community, and to build bridges?

Jesus also says, "Do you think that I have come to bring peace to the earth? No, I tell you, but rather division! From now on, five in one household will be divided, three against two and two against three" (Lk 12:51–52). What do I do with all these harsh words? Isn't there enough religious conflict? Isn't Jesus inciting me here to a confrontational life and stirring me up to create separation between people? I still remember Pasolini's movie *The Gospel According to St. Matthew.* There Jesus is portrayed as an intense, angry rebel who alienates everyone in sight.

I have made an inner decision to keep looking at Jesus as the one who calls us to the heart of God, a heart that knows only love. It is from that perspective that I reflect on everything Jesus says, including his harsh statements. Jesus created divisions, but I have chosen to believe that these divisions were the result not of intolerance or fanaticism but of his radical call to love, forgive, and be reconciled.

Every time I have an opportunity to create understanding between people and foster moments of healing, forgiving, and uniting, I will try to do it, even though I might be criticized as too soft, too bending, too appeasing. Is this desire a lack of fervor and zeal for the truth? Is it an unwillingness to be a martyr? Is it spinelessness? I am not always sure what comes from my weakness and what comes from my strength. Probably I will never know. But I have to trust that, after sixty-four years of life, I have some ground to stand on, a ground where Jesus stands with me.

And when divisions arise against my desire, I have to find the courage to live them as lovingly as I tried to prevent them; then Jesus' harsh words might prove consoling.

Friday, March 15

Last night I watched a television conversation between Bill Moyers and Joseph Campbell. It was a rerun of a series of programs made in the eighties.

I was struck by Campbell's remark that we serve the world by being spiritually well. The first questions are not: "How much do we do?" or "How many people do we help out?" but "Are we interiorly at peace?" Campbell confirmed my own conviction that the distinction between contemplation and action can be misleading. Jesus' actions flowed from his interior communion with God. His presence was healing, and it changed the world. In a sense he didn't do anything! "Everyone who touched him was healed" (Mk 6:56).

This morning during the Eucharist we discussed the great commandment. The same theme came up. When we love God with all our heart, mind, strength, and soul, we cannot do other than love our neighbor, and our very selves. It is by being fully rooted in the heart of God that we are creatively connected with our neighbor as well as with our deepest self. In the heart of God we can see that the other human beings who live on this earth with us are also God's sons and daughters, and belong to the same family we do. There too I can recognize and claim my own belovedness, and celebrate it with my neighbors.

Our society thinks economically: "How much love do I give to God, how much to my neighbor, and how much to myself?" But God says, "Give all your love to me, and I will give you your neighbor and yourself."

We are not talking here about moral obligations or ethical imperatives. We are talking about the mystical life. It is the intimate communion with God that reveals to us how to live in the world and act in God's Name.

Saturday, March 16

In one of Jesus' stories a Pharisee, standing by himself, prays to God: "God, I thank you that I am not like other people" (Lk 18:11).

That's a prayer we often pray. "I'm glad I'm not like him, her, or them. I am lucky not to belong to that family, that country, or that race. I am blessed not to be part of that company, that team, or that crowd!" Most of this prayer is unceasing! Somewhere we are always comparing ourselves with others, trying to convince ourselves that we are better off than they are. It is a prayer that wells up from our fearful selves and guides many of our thoughts and actions.

But this is a very dangerous prayer. It leads from compassion to competition, from competition to rivalry, from rivalry to violence, from violence to war, from war to destruction. It is a prayer that lies all the time, because we are not the difference we try so hard to find. No, our deepest identity is rooted where we are like other people — weak, broken, sinful, but sons and daughters of God.

I even think that we should not thank God for not being like other creatures, animals, plants, or rocks! We should thank God that indeed we are like them, not better or worse but integral parts of God's creation. This is what humility is all about. We belong to the humus, the soil, and it is in this belonging that we can find the deepest reason for gratitude. Our prayer must be, "Thank you, God, that I am worthy to be part of your creation. Be merciful to me a sinner." Through this prayer we will be justified (see Lk 18:14), that is, find our just place in God's Kingdom.

Sunday, March 17

To the question who was to blame for the tragedy of a man born blind, Jesus replied, Nobody. "He was born blind so that God's works might be revealed in him" (Jn 9:3).

We spend a lot of energy wondering who can be blamed for our own or other people's tragedies — our parents, ourselves, the immigrants, the Jews, the gays, the blacks, the fundamentalists, the Catholics? There is a strange satisfaction in being able to point our finger at someone, even ourselves. It gives us some sort of explanation and offers us some form of clarity.

But Jesus doesn't allow us to solve our own or other people's problems through blame. The challenge he poses is to discern in the midst of our darkness the light of God. In Jesus' vision everything, even the greatest tragedy, can become an occasion in which God's works can be revealed.

How radically new my life would be if I were willing to move beyond blaming to proclaiming the works of God in our midst. I don't think it has much to do with the exterior of life. All human beings have their tragedies — death, depression, betrayal, rejection, poverty, separation, loss, and so on. We seldom have much control over them. But do we choose to live them as occasions to blame, or as occasions to see God at work?

The whole Hebrew Bible is a story of human tragedies, but when these tragedies are lived and remembered as the context in which God's unconditional love for the people of Israel is revealed, this story becomes sacred history.

Tuesday, March 19

Today is the Feast of St. Joseph, the righteous man. Often the family of Jesus is portrayed as the model for all families. But a closer look at the way Joseph, Mary, and Jesus lived together evokes little desire for imitation. Indeed, Joseph was a very decent man. He didn't want to give his pregnant girlfriend a bad reputation, and after a reassuring dream, he married her. But was it a happy life? When Jesus was twelve they lost him in the crowd, and when they found him, after three days of anxiously looking, their question: "Why did you do this to us?" was answered with something close to a reproach: "Did you not know that I must be in my Father's house?" (Lk 2:49). This response, "But didn't you know I have more important things to do than pay attention to you," is hardly consoling.

All the other references to Jesus' family life are more disturbing than consoling. At Cana when Mary asks for his help, Jesus says, "What do you want from me? My hour has not come yet" (Jn 2:4). When, later, Jesus receives a message saying, "Look, your mother and brothers and sisters are outside asking for you," he replies, "Who are my mother and my brothers?" (Mk 3:32–33). Finally we find Mary standing under the cross. Seeing his mother and his beloved disciple, John, Jesus says to his mother, "Woman, this is your son" (Jn 19:27). About Joseph there is no word. What happened to him? Did he die?

In this time of broken families, of separation and divorce, of children with only one parent, and of mothers and fathers in great anxiety about their suicidal or drug-using kids, the seemingly quite dysfunctional family of Jesus may offer us some solace! It is clear to me that Jesus is quite ambivalent if not negative about so-called family values such as family harmony, filial affection, staying together at all costs. I wonder if our church's elevation of celibacy, especially for those who want to serve God, does not have its roots in the quite disturbing situation of Jesus' own family.

But Joseph is a saint! He lived it all in a great hiddenness. Ignored by the Gospel writers and by the early church, he emerges today as a man trusting in God even when there was hardly anything for him to hold on to.

Wednesday, March 20

These days I feel strong, alive, and full of energy. Still, I am aware that much of that well-being is the direct result of the loving support of many friends. At the moment I do not experience any anger or hostility directed toward me. I feel in gentle harmony with my family, the people in Daybreak, especially Nathan and Sue, and the many friends close by and far away. In situations like this I easily forget how fragile I am inside, and how little is needed to throw me off balance. A small rejection, a slight criticism might be enough to make me doubt my self-worth and even lose my self-confidence.

I had been thinking about this when I read Michelangelo's poems to Tommaso Cavalieri, the young Roman nobleman whom he first met in 1532, when he was fifty-seven years old. His love for Tommaso, and Tommaso's affection for him, made him feel fully alive. He writes:

> With your bright eyes, I see the living light which my blind eyes alone can never see; and your sure feet take up that load for me which my lame gait would let fall helplessly. My very thoughts are framed within your heart.

These words evoke deep feelings in me. They reveal my true dependence on human affection and love. I know how many of my thoughts are framed in the hearts of those who love me.

Thursday, March 21

The first day of spring. It still is chilly, cloudy, and wet, and the heat is still on in the house. But at least there is the promise of new color, new sunshine, new leaves on the trees. I can't wait to see it all happen.

Sunday, March 24

The resurrection of Lazarus is one of the most complex stories of the New Testament. It has many levels of meaning. This morning I found myself speaking about it without always fully knowing on which level I was moving.

First of all, there is the contrast between the death threat against Jesus and the calling to life of Lazarus. When Jesus says to his disciples, "Lazarus is dead. For your sake I am glad I was not there, so that you may believe. But let us go to him," Thomas says to his fellow disciples, "Let us also go, that we may die with him" (Jn 11:14–16). Going to Lazarus meant going to Judea, where Jesus' enemies were trying to kill him. But going to Lazarus also meant going to the place of life. The resurrection of Lazarus becomes the event where death and life touch each other. After Lazarus was called back to life, the leaders became determined to kill Jesus (Jn 11:53). All of this can be seen as Jesus' way of preparing his friends and disciples for his own death and resurrection. By resurrecting Lazarus, Jesus shows that he is indeed the resurrection (Jn 11:25) and that his own death, which will happen soon, is not a final death.

Second, there is a love story here. Lazarus was one of Jesus' closest friends, and his deep compassion for Lazarus's sisters, as well as his great love for Lazarus, moved Jesus to call Lazarus back to life. Whenever Jesus calls someone to life — the son of the widow of Nain, the daughter of Jairus — we always see an immense love and compassion. It is this love and compassion that is the source of new life.

Third, there are Jesus' words when he first heard of Lazarus's illness: "This illness does not lead to death; rather it is for God's glory, so that the Son of God may be glorified through it" (Jn 11:4). As in many other situations Jesus sees a tragic event as the opportunity to reveal God's glory.

How do all these levels belong together? Maybe the best way to answer that question is to look at Jesus' own death and resurrection. There we see that the final power of death is overcome. There we see that this overcoming of death takes place in the context of love of those who knew Jesus intimately. There we see the greatest tragedy of human history become the occasion for the salvation of the world.

Thursday, March 28

During the Eucharist this morning we talked about God's covenant. God says, "I am your God and will be faithful to you even when you won't be faithful to me." Through human history, this divine faithfulness is shown to us in God's increasing desire for intimacy. At first God was the God *for* us, our protector and shield. Then, when Jesus came, God became the God *with* us, our companion and friend. Finally, when Jesus sent his Spirit, God was revealed to us as the God *within* us, our very breath and heartbeat.

Saturday, March 30

At 3:30 p.m. Sue, Carl, and John arrived by bus in Bernards-ville. They were in a good mood and quite happy with the miniretreat they had given.

. . . Today I received news that Claire, a friend of mine, had died. I had hoped to visit her because I knew that she was ailing and now I am sorry that I did not get there. Quite a few years ago, Claire had come to Daybreak to ask for some spiritual support. She had been struggling with deep feelings of rejection and depression and had been seeing a psychiatrist for many years without much result. Although she had lived in "high society" and had known many of "the great" of our world, she often felt very lonely and even unappreciated. Underneath it all was the question: "Do people really love me for who I am?"

Sue and I had both talked with her several times during her visit, but what really deeply affected her was her dinner at the New House, where she met Adam, Rosie, John, Michael, Bill, and their assistants. It was a completely new world for her. During her time at the New House, something happened within her that had a radical effect on her inner life. She felt accepted for who she was. Nobody there knew about her life, her notoriety, her fortune, or her many connections. She was simply Claire, but the people around the table made her feel that she was special to them.

After her visit to Daybreak I called Claire often and visited her several times. Every time she said again, "At Daybreak my depression left me. I have many problems with my health and I often have to go to the hospital, but I know now that God is close to me and that I am loved."

Now Claire is dead. Her body was finally no longer able to hold on to her spirit. I am glad she had such an easy death, without long suffering. She died at peace with God, her husband, her children, and her many friends. Her daughter asked me to celebrate the Eucharist and give the homily at her funeral. I hope and pray that the many people who will be there will get a glimpse of the immense love of God that Claire experienced through the broken people of Daybreak.

Watertown, Sunday, March 31

After a very animated Palm Sunday Eucharist in the living room, with about twenty people, and a pancake breakfast at Peggy's home, Peggy drove Nathan, Sue, Carl, John, and me to Newark Airport. Shortly after Nathan, Sue, Carl, and John left for Toronto, I was on my way to Boston.

In Boston, Jonas was waiting at the airport. It was really good to see him again. The main purpose of my visit was to be part of an evening at St. Paul's Catholic Church in Cambridge to celebrate Jonas's book, *Rebecca*.

It was a beautiful evening. Close to five hundred people came. Both Jonas and I gave short presentations about the loss of a child and the journey from grief to gratitude. This being the first day of Holy Week allowed us to make the evening into a spiritual preparation for entering deeply into the paschal mystery. We sang several Taizé songs. Jonas played two pieces on his flute, and after a short intermission several people spoke about their own pain connected with the loss of a child, a family member, or a friend.

One woman touched me very deeply. She told us that long ago she had given up her baby son for adoption because of the shame of being pregnant without being married. Twenty years later, while trying to get in touch with her son, she discovered that he had died in an accident when he was eight years old. Upon hearing this she experienced an immense sense of loss and grief. But gradually she was able to live through her pain. The experience brought her to study theology, and today she is close to getting her master of divinity degree.

This and many other stories made the evening special. We concluded with a prayer and the Our Father. Many people stayed after the presentations, talking to one another. All of Jonas's books at the church were sold.

It was a wonderful evening. I felt very grateful to be there with Margaret, Jonas, and many old friends. There was a spirit of love and joy in the midst of the tears that were shed. I was especially happy because Margaret and Jonas shared their feelings about Rebecca and they were so available during the question and answer time.

April 1996

New York, Monday, April 1

At 6:00 p.m. Krister and his wife, Brita, came for dinner at Jonas and Margaret's home. Krister, while Dean of Harvard Divinity School, had invited me to join the faculty. I had accepted his invitation, but shortly after I came to Harvard, he became the Lutheran bishop of Stockholm. When Krister and Brita returned to Cambridge after four years in Stockholm, I had left to join L'Arche. Krister may have felt a little guilty about getting me to Harvard, because he knew that my time there had been quite hard for me, and in many ways disappointing.

I was happy to have the opportunity to tell him that there was no bitterness in me about my time at Harvard, and that there was no reason for him to feel guilty. I told him that during my three years at Harvard I had made some beautiful friends, especially Jonas and Margaret. I said I had discovered that although the academic life had been a good life for me, my deep desire was for a life with the poor in a community with a contemplative dimension. Without Harvard I wonder if I ever would have been able to choose for L'Arche. It was a real joy for me to reestablish my friendship with Krister and Brita after a twelve-year interruption.

At 9:00 p.m. Jonas drove me to the airport. By 11:45 p.m. I had arrived at Wendy and Jay's home in New York. I am a little nervous about Claire's funeral tomorrow.

Richmond Hill, Tuesday, April 2

A little before 9:00 a.m. I arrived at the church for Claire's funeral. The sanctuary was nearly full by the time the casket was brought in. The liturgy was very gentle in mood. In the homily I spoke about Claire's poverty — her wounded heart searching for love — and about the blessings she received. I tried to express how her real blessings were hidden, not in her fame, wealth, or success but in her little, often lonely heart.

At 2:00 p.m. I was on my way back to Toronto to celebrate Holy Week and Easter with my community. When I arrived at Daybreak, Sue, Carl, Nathan and his parents, from Calgary, joined us for dinner at the Dayspring. It is very good to be back home again.

Wednesday, April 3

A busy day with work in the office, several planning meetings, dinner at the Church Street House, and other events. But what dominated my day emotionally was news of the suicide of a man that I barely knew.

The first time I had met him, about four years ago, his kindness had touched me in a deep way. In the following years I lost contact with him, but I was grateful to see him turn up at a lecture recently. He looked very good, in fact, open and radiant. We embraced, and I said, "It's so good to see you again after all these years." There were so many people crowding around us at the moment that that was all I could say.

The next day I realized that I had no plans for lunch, so I had called his home but all I got was the answering machine. I didn't know his work number, so I left a message hoping that someone would pick it up and let him know that I was free for lunch. Nothing happened.

Last night his friend Vincent called and told me that he had committed suicide on Monday afternoon by jumping from the roof of a building.

My whole interior flooded. I didn't even know what to think or feel, but I was overwhelmed. What had happened? Why did he kill himself? Where was his partner? And, beyond all these quick, stormy thoughts, there was the sense of loss: he is gone. I will never see him again, never get to know him. His young life so full of promise is cut off, suddenly, desperately. I hardly knew him, but he had touched me and I remembered him well. I had not been aware of any depression, inner anguish, or despair. He had looked so well on the night of the lecture. He had seemed so attentive and free. When a woman in a wheelchair wasn't able to reach the lecture hall, he was there to offer his help. There was no sign of self-absorption or inner pain. Now he is gone, forever. My heart turns, turns, turns. . . .

Tonight I talked to his partner for nearly an hour. He was deeply shocked but able not to let his grief overwhelm him. He told me about their long relationship. He told me about his friend's long struggle with depression, how he had often spoken about his desire to kill himself, about his many fears, especially about being a disappointment to others. He told me that last year during Holy Week he had attempted to kill himself by jumping from the same building.

I just listened. It was a story of love and pain, communion and separation, intimacy and distance. So strange! This was someone that I saw only twice, but he rooted himself somewhere in my heart.

Holy Thursday, April 4

The whole community met at 2:00 p.m. in St. Mary's Anglican Church for the foot-washing service, and again at 8:00 p.m. we came together in the Dayspring chapel to celebrate the Eucharist. Daniel, the youngest son of one of the Daybreak families, received his first communion.

I carry in my heart a jumble of images: many, many people, young and old, strong and weak, happy and depressed — talking, asking, laughing, crying — confessing their sins, expressing their gratitude, kissing, hugging, singing, washing each other's feet, listening to words of reassurance, receiving the Body and Blood of Jesus — giving gifts, decorating, flowers in vases, wheelchairs, purple and white vestments and robes — Holy Thursday, Claire and her grieving family, Peggy and Phil, Jonas — Holy, Holy week, leading to Easter — pain in the world, plane accidents, murders and tragedies — a big snowstorm, slippery road — having dinner with friends — Kathy and Timmy waiting for her baby soon — little Daniel, beautiful eyes, eager to receive Jesus, and many presents, especially a watch, knowing all about the Son of God and the Son of Mary, who died for us and rose from the grave — many children listening, getting distracted — community, friendship, fund-raising and planning, the architect, new buildings — calling home to Holland. Phone calls from publishers, letters with invitations to come here and there to speak, just to be present, to write forewords and recommendations — Holy Thursday, Holy Week — Peace, Joy, Hope, Trust — God and all the people — just one day, only one day.

Good Friday, April 5

About a hundred of us walked from the meeting hall to the Dayspring chapel, each carrying a stone to symbolize our burden and our brokenness. We stopped three times to remember how Jesus is condemned to death, Simon of Cyrene is forced to carry the cross when Jesus falls, and Veronica wipes Jesus' face with her towel. Jesus is nailed to the cross.

147

Michael, Adam's brother, dressed in an alb and with a crown of thorns on his head, is Jesus. An assistant helps him to carry the cross. At the third station there is an armchair for him to rest in. We sing and listen to reflections on the passion of Jesus. In the chapel we place our stones on or around the cross. Sitting together in chairs and on the floor we sing, "Behold, behold, the wood of the cross." Lorenzo hammers three big nails in the cross, piercing the silence. Then we sing again: "Were you there when they crucified my Lord?... Were you there when they nailed him to the tree?... Were you there when they laid him in the tomb?... Sometimes it causes me to tremble, tremble, tremble."

Yes, it is a good Friday. In the midst of all the grief and mourning, there is sweet consolation. We are together, and there is love pouring out from our broken hearts and from the pierced heart of God.

Tonight we met again to listen to John's story of Jesus' passion, to pray for the church and the world, to venerate the cross, and to receive communion. The cross is in the center. As I look at the large crucifix, I remember how it came to us. Four years ago a Franciscan priest, Father Pancratius, whom I met in Freiburg while he was dying of cancer, said to me, "Henri, I want to give you this crucifix before I die. I want you to give it a place among your people with disabilities."

He told me the story of the crucifix. When many years ago he went to Croatia with a group of young Germans to help restore a church that was destroyed during World War II, they found the crucifix under the rubble. The pastor, grateful for the German gesture of reconciliation, gave it to Father Pancratius. There were no crossbeams, just the wood-carved body. When the dying priest gave it to me for my community, I felt as if I had been given a mandate to connect the suffering that comes from hatred, violence, and war with the suffering of people with physical and mental disabilities.

Joe, the leader of Daybreak's woodworking shop, The Woodery, together with the men with disabilities who work with him — Bill, John, David, Gordie — made two large, finely polished crossbeams on which the body was hung. For three years now the large cross has been on the wall of the vestibule of the Dayspring chapel. Today we brought the cross into the chapel and placed it on the lap of Michael, who was resting in his beanbag. Michael, who has severe cerebral palsy, was glad to "hold" the cross and let people come to it to pray. Michael's spastic body and the body of Jesus on the cross became like one body. As people formed a line to kiss the feet of Jesus on the cross, they realized that Jesus continues to suffer until the end of time in the countless people whose hearts and bodies are broken.

Good Friday is much more than reliving the passion of Jesus; it is entering into solidarity with the passion of all the people of our planet, whether in the past, the present, or the future. In Jesus all human suffering is collected. The broken heart of Jesus is the broken heart of God. The broken heart of God is the broken heart of the world. "Behold, behold, the wood of the cross on which is hung our salvation. Oh, come let us adore."

Holy Saturday, April 6

Most of the day I spent preparing — with other members of the community — for the Easter Vigil celebration. As we all gathered, we were ready: flowers, music, decorations. The little basement chapel was packed to capacity as we brought in the Easter candle, listened to the readings, renewed our baptismal vows, and celebrated the Eucharist.

After the Gospel reading I reflected on the significance of our faith in the resurrection of the body. As a community of people conscious of our disabilities, we are held together not so much by the Word as by the body. Although we use many words and there is a lot of "talk" among us, it is the weak bodies of our core members that create community. We wash, shave, comb, dress, clean, feed, and hold the bodies of those who are entrusted to us and thus build a communal body. As we claim our faith in the resurrection of the body, we come to see that the resurrection is not simply an event after death but a reality of everyday life. Our care for the body calls us to unity beyond organization, to intimacy beyond eroticism, and to integrity beyond psychological wholeness.

Unity, intimacy, and integrity are the three spiritual qualities of the resurrected life. We are called to break through the boundaries of nationality, race, sexual orientation, age, and mental capacities and create a unity of love that allows the weakest among us to live well. We are called to go far beyond the places of lust, sexual need, and desire for physical union to a spiritual intimacy that involves body, mind, and heart. And we are called to let go of old ways of feeling good about ourselves and reach out to a new integration of the many facets of our humanity. These calls are calls to the resurrection. Caring for the body is preparing the body for the final resurrection while anticipating it in our daily lives through spiritual unity, intimacy, and integrity.

As I talked about these things it seemed that those who were present at the vigil could recognize some of what I spoke about in their daily Daybreak life.

As we received the Body and Blood of Jesus, I was struck by the *real* quality of the paschal mystery. We are the people of the resurrection, living our lives with a great vision that transforms us as we are living it.

Easter Sunday, April 7

"Christ is risen. He is risen indeed." We whisper it to each other. We joyfully announce it. We shout it from the rooftops. It was a very colorful and happy celebration this morning. Brian and Nathan played their guitars and led us in song. The small children opened the cocoons, which, on Ash Wednesday they had filled with things we want to let go of and things we hope for, and we all admired the butterflies that came out.

And the flowers were so radiant, especially the flowers that covered the large wooden cross Michael had carried on Good Friday. After we had sung our hearts out with Glorias and Alleluias, we all — more than a hundred of us — had an Easter brunch that began with "Christ is risen" in at least ten languages. It all was exuberant, festive, and very exciting.

Then in the afternoon Nathan, his parents, and I went to see the Dutch film *Antonia's Line*. What a contrast! All the issues that haunt our contemporary world were there. Violence, sexual abuse, murderous revenge, accidents, suicide, irrelevant religion, and cynicism were all part of Antonia's life. In and through it there is Antonia, a stoic woman who faces it and chooses her own moment to die, bravely, but without a glimpse of Him who rose from the tomb. For me *Antonia's Line* was a meeting with my own country, culture, and history, especially after the jubilant morning celebration in Canada. I felt like I was in my two homes, L'Arche and Holland, on the same Easter Day. Both the risen Lord and Antonia live within me, and somehow I have to come to love them both. The cover of *Time* magazine this week shows the face of Jesus, half of it holy, half of it sensual, and the cover story wonders whether the resurrection is a fable or a divine truth. All of this is very close to me. I realize that my faith and unbelief are never far from each other. Maybe it is exactly at the place where they touch each other that the growing edge of my life is. . . .

Easter Tuesday, April 9

A beautiful Easter Tuesday Eucharist at 9:00 a.m., with good conversation about the resurrection, shopping in the morning for office supplies and food, mailing things, sleeping in the afternoon, dinner with Peggy and Phil in the evening, telephone calls, faxes, and so on.

Today I was thinking how nobody recognizes Jesus immediately. They think he is the gardener, a stranger, or a ghost. But when a familiar gesture is there again — breaking bread, inviting the disciples to try for another catch, calling them by name — his friends know he is there with them. Absence and presence are touching each other. The old Jesus is gone. They no longer can be with him as before. The new Jesus, the risen Lord, is there, more intimately than ever. It is an empowering presence. "Do not cling to me . . . but go . . . and tell" (Jn 20:17).

The resurrection stories reveal the always-present tension between coming and leaving, intimacy and distance, holding and letting go, at-homeness and mission, presence and absence. We face that tension every day. It puts us on the journey to the full realization of the promise given to us. "Do not cling to me" might mean "This is not heaven yet" but also "I am now within you and empower you for a spiritual task in the world, continuing what I have begun. You are the living Christ."

While many question whether the resurrection really took place, I wonder if it doesn't take place every day if we have the eyes to see and the ears to hear.

Easter Wednesday, April 10

Several interesting letters today. A friend of mine wrote to tell me about attending a Eucharist that I celebrated with Bill, from Daybreak, assisting me. While at first my friend felt repulsed by Bill's disability, appearance, and behavior, she finally received communion from him and was deeply moved by the look of love and compassion in his eyes. All of this must have taken place at least four years ago, but the letter was written in 1996. A true grace.

Then there was a long letter from Rodleigh of the Flying Rodleighs, full of stories about all that had happened to them since we last saw each other in Holland. Lots of setbacks — cold weather, poor health, failing trapeze tricks, car trouble, and so on. But, as always, Rodleigh remains optimistic and looks forward to a better summer. I look forward to seeing them again in July.

Thursday, April 11

Most of the day I have been busy preparing for my ten-day trip that starts tomorrow — Newark, Chicago, San Francisco, Cleveland, Chicago, Newark. I am looking forward to the several events: Don's birthday, visiting Jeff and Maurice, discussing the book of daily meditations with the publishers, a few days with Frank, Alvaro, and Kevin, preaching at the installation of Jim in Cleveland, and leading a workshop about the inclusion of people with disabilities in the liturgy. It is going to be work as well as vacation.

Chicago, Friday, April 12

When I arrived in Chicago, Don was waiting for me. Twenty minutes later Claude arrived from Portland.

I have known both Don and Claude since 1966, when I came to the University of Notre Dame as a visiting professor in the Psychology Department. Our thirty-year friendship has been very important for us in our personal as well as our professional journeys. Don's sixtieth birthday gave him the excuse to invite both Claude and me for a quiet day at his father's summer house before his birthday party at his father's home in Winnetka. I am really glad to be with Don and Claude and to reflect on our past and future as we enter the "third phase" of our lives.

Tuesday, April 16

The Easter issue of *Time* magazine had as its cover article a discussion about the "quest for the historical Jesus." In recent years Harper has published three books on the subject: *Jesus: A Revolutionary Biography* by John Dominic Crossan, *Meeting Jesus Again for the First Time*, by Marcus J. Borg, and *The Real Jesus* by Luke Timothy Johnson. John gave me the three books yesterday, and I have been reading them off and on, here and there.

These books force me to ask again, "Who is Jesus for me?" and "What does it mean when I say: I believe in Jesus?" I very much like what Johnson writes in his conclusion when he talks about the "real Jesus" being "first of all the powerful, resurrected Lord whose transforming spirit is active in the community." But the "real Jesus" also reproduces in our lives a faithful obedience to God as well as loving service to others. Then Borg says "that we cannot understand or explain the post-Easter Jesus by historical facts only because the post-Easter Jesus is the Jesus of tradition and *experience*."

Reading these studies I experience a deep desire to write more about the meaning and significance of Jesus for my own and other people's daily lives. This year, more than ever, the Gospel stories about the resurrection have deepened my hope and faith and have given me a new vision of the body. Crossan, Borg, and Johnson all have helped me but most of all challenged me to make the true connection between the story of Jesus and our stories.

Oakland, California,
Friday, April 19

Michael, a longtime friend and founder-coordinator of Bethany House, a small Catholic Worker house for people with AIDS, joined us on our return to Oakland. My plan was to spend the afternoon and evening with him.

The unexpected surprise of today was that Andrew Harvey, the specialist on Rumi and writer on mysticism, was giving a lecture. It was, for me, an opportunity to meet this spiritual writer, whose life and work have intrigued me from the moment I first heard about him. Tom, a Franciscan priest and friend of Michael, joined us.

The lecture was excellent, and I was moved by it, not just because of its content but because of Andrew's transparent, radiant, free, humorful, and bright presence. Everything about him — the way he looked at his audience, took his glasses off and put them on again, and directed his questions to his listeners as an invitation to personal transformation in which both radical love for God and radical service for others were asked for — made me want to know this "messenger."

After the lecture I introduced myself to him. It seemed that he had never heard of me until he realized that I was the author of *Life of the Beloved*. Then he reacted with excitement. "I have your book right beside my bed, and I read in it very often. I like your style, the way you write about suffering, and the nice size of your books. We should meet." I never asked an author for an autograph before, but now I said, "Please sign your book for me, and let me know where I can write you and send you a few of my own books. . . . "

Peapack, Tuesday, April 23

After a one-hour delay I left Chicago late this morning and got to Newark at 1:30 p.m. Peggy was there to take me back to Peapack. We had a lot to tell each other about our "adventures" during the past week. Back in my little red house I spent most of the afternoon reading and answering mail, listening to voice messages, and making phone calls.

Wednesday, April 24

Tonight at 8:00 p.m. Timmy called to tell me about the birth of his new sister, Sarah. She was born at noon on Monday morning. "I cut the umbilical cord," Timmy said quite proudly. I wondered how it must feel for a ten-year-old boy to see his sister appear from his mother's womb. When I was twelve and my second brother was born, I had no idea how that happened. All I remember are cakes, flowers, a nice-smelling room, a little, beautifully dressed baby in a large crib, my mother in bed but clearly not sick, and many visitors. As a young boy, it seemed to me that my father hadn't much place in it all. When he came home from work he had another son! But that was another time and another place!

Kathy came to the phone and told me that the birth had gone well. "Timmy was wonderful," she said. "When I had no energy anymore to push, he said, 'Come on, Mom, you can do it!'" I look forward to seeing Sarah on Friday when I return to Daybreak. I am happy to be Sarah's godfather.

Richmond Hill, Friday, April 26

After the Eucharist in Peapack with a very lively discussion about the story of Paul's conversion, I got ready to leave again for Toronto.

The two reasons for returning to Daybreak are the meeting of the Dayspring Council and the celebration of Nathan's community leadership for the coming four years. During the past five years the Daybreak community has been planning to build a new Dayspring or spiritual center, which will include a house of hospitality and a new chapel. The present Dayspring building is a small bungalow with five bedrooms and a large basement converted into a chapel. With more than 150 members, the Daybreak community needs more space to pray and to offer hospitality. The Dayspring Council is a small group of people from Toronto and several places in the USA who oversee the project, offer suggestions, and participate in the ongoing fund-raising.

At 8:00 p.m. the community gathered in the Dayspring chapel for the Eucharist. Kathy, Timmy, and four-day-old Sarah were there. What a tiny and beautiful baby. It was Sarah's first visit to the chapel. She will be there often! After the homily I gave Sarah a special blessing.

It is good to be back in Daybreak. It will be a very busy weekend with the council meeting, Nathan's installation, and discussions with the architect. I hope it will be life giving and hope giving.

Saturday, April 27

The Dayspring Council meeting was very encouraging and unifying. There were many questions and an overall excitement about the plans and the way they fitted in the general vision of the Daybreak community.

I concluded the day with a visit to Kathy, Timmy, and little Sarah.

Sunday, April 28

Having completed one four-year term as community leader, Nathan was asked and agreed to continue in the role for another four years. This afternoon the whole Daybreak community gathered in the meeting hall to celebrate his leadership. It was an afternoon of affirmation, celebration, and encouragement, with songs, speeches, skits, and many blessings.

In my own little presentation I took two triangles, one with the point up and the other with the point down. Nathan is boss but also shepherd, a leader who gives direction but also a leader who listens, a man who talks with the government, is concerned about budgets, and connects our agency with other agencies, but also a man who holds us together as community, prays with us, joins us at the table, and keeps our focus on those who are the weakest among us. The triangle with the point up shows that we are *in* the world as an agency not afraid of competition. The triangle with the point down shows that

160

we are not *of* the world, but we are a community of service and care.

After explaining these two triangles, I put them on top of each other so that together they formed a star. I believe that it is precisely the tension between the upward and the downward triangles that creates the light, a guiding and enlightening light. It is very hard these days to be a good leader, prudent as a snake and gentle as a dove, but Nathan has a unique ability.

Peapack, Monday, April 29

A very busy day. A morning Eucharist in the Dayspring chapel with close to fifty people, dictating letters to Kathy, visiting the doctor in Richmond Hill to unplug my ears, lunch with Joe, a three-hour meeting with the architect about the plans to build a small house for me connected to the present Dayspring, a visit to the New House for a chat with the assistants about Adam's death and their own plans for the future....

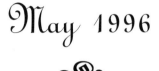

May 1996

Wednesday, May 1

This afternoon Frank was promoted in the U.S. Air Force. It was a very important event for him. Regrettably none of his family or friends could be there with him. Part of the problem was that the promotion took place during a week of exercises on the base, and there was no time for celebrations. Still, I wished I could have been there for Frank. There are not too many special occasions in his life, and this public affirmation of his ministry needs to be celebrated. Hopefully we can do it in the future.

When we were in Santa Fe, Frank asked me, "Could you write a prayer for me for my promotion?" I said, "Sure," but later wondered whether he wanted a prayer that I prayed for him or a prayer that he himself could pray. When I finally wrote the prayer, I felt drawn to make it a prayer that he could pray, not only once but often. I tried to crawl into his skin and speak to God from his heart. Frank is not a man of many words, especially words that connect with his feelings. That probably is the main reason why I chose to pray in his name. So this is the prayer I wrote:

Dear Lord,

As I come to the halfway point of my life, I want to enter into your presence and recommit myself to you. During the last four decades, you have guided me and gradually brought me to a mature faith, to a new confidence in my gifts, and to a spiritual adulthood. Along the way I have struggled with many things, trying to find my place in life, trying to find my place in my family, trying to find my place among my colleagues, trying to find my place as your minister. It has been a long journey with many joys and many pains, with many doubts and many hopes, with many moments of loneliness and with moments of beautiful friendship.

Now, as I receive the affirmation of my colleagues in being promoted to the rank of major in the U.S. Air Force, I come again to ask you to lead me always closer to your heart, and to the hearts of those who are entrusted to me. Precisely because I find myself in a secure place, with good health and good friends, I am free to choose you again as my shepherd and my guide. Help me to be humble in the midst of a world that is so full of ambition. Help me to be vulnerable in a world so concerned with power. Help me to be simple in surroundings that are so complicated. Help me to be forgiving in a society where revenge and retaliation create so much pain. Help me to be poor of spirit in a milieu that desires so many riches and aspires to so much success. As I enter the second half of my life, I come to you with an open heart, asking that I may trust in the gifts you have given me and may have the courage to take risks in your service.

I do not know where you will lead me. I do not know where I will be two, five, or ten years from now. I do not know the road ahead of me, but I know now that you are with me to guide me and that, wherever you lead me, even where I would rather not go, you will bring me closer to my true home. Thank you, Lord, for my life, for my vocation, and for the hope that you have planted in my heart. Amen.

Saturday, May 4

For some reason I feel quite anxious interiorly. I realize that I am walking around with some deep, unresolved emotions and that not much is needed to bring them to the surface and throw me off balance. I wasn't expecting this, but I feel quite powerless in the face of these free-floating emotions of love, hate, rejection, attraction, gratitude, and regret. I wish I could come to a new peace, but after so many years I fear that new tensions instead of peace may be in store. I know that prayer is very important at this moment.

Monday, May 6

We are waiting for the Spirit to come. Are we really? This morning during the Eucharist I spoke a little about preparing ourselves for Pentecost just as we prepare ourselves for Christmas and Easter. Still, for most of us Pentecost is a non-event. While on secular calendars Christmas and Easter are still marked, Pentecost is spectacularly absent.

But Pentecost is the coming of the Spirit of Jesus into the world. It is the celebration of God breaking through the boundaries of time and space and opening the whole world for the re-creating power of love. Pentecost is freedom, the freedom of the Spirit to blow where it wants.

Without Pentecost the Christ-event — the life, death, and resurrection of Jesus — remains imprisoned in history as something to remember, think about, and reflect on. The Spirit of Jesus comes to dwell within us, so that we can become living Christs here and now. Pentecost lifts the whole mystery of salvation out of its particularities and makes it into something universal, embracing all peoples, all countries, all seasons, and all eras. Pentecost is also the moment of empowering. Each individual human being can claim the Spirit of Jesus as the guiding spirit of his or her life. In that Spirit we can speak and act freely and confidently with the knowledge that the same Spirit that inspired Jesus is inspiring us.

We certainly have to prepare ourselves carefully for this feast so that we can not only receive fully the gifts of the Spirit but also let the Spirit bear fruit within us.

Tuesday, May 7

This morning during the Eucharist, Don left a message on the phone telling me that his father had died in the night. I immediately called him, and we spoke about Don Sr.'s beautiful life and peaceful death. This is a great loss for Don and his family. Don really loved his father and during the last few years had grown very close to him.

I am so glad that I was with Don Sr. ["Himself"] only three weeks ago. Weak as he was, he clearly was the quiet center of the family, and always with a prayer and a smile. Without any doubt he was a great human being. He was a very good husband, a greatly admired father, a generous supporter of the poor and the weak, and a man of deep faith. To me he was always a most gracious host, always interested in my life and work, always supporting my writing, and always eager to pray with me and Don. I will truly miss him.

On Thursday I will fly to Chicago to be at the wake and the funeral. I just want to be close to Don during this time of grief and mourning.

Winnetka, Illinois, Thursday, May 9

I arrived at O'Hare Airport at 6:00 p.m. and immediately found a cab to take me to the funeral home in Skokie.

I knelt in front of the closed casket that held Don Sr.'s body and prayed. My prayers were more *to* Himself than *for* Himself. As I let my head rest on the casket, I asked Don Sr. to send me his spirit of equanimity, kindness, and humor, and to guide me in the years ahead. I especially prayed to him to intercede with Jesus to take my inner anguish away and to lead me to a greater inner peace. I also asked to be a good, faithful friend to Don, his brothers, and their aunt in their grief.

Peapack, Monday, May 13

I am glad to be home again. Now I can dedicate the whole week to writing about Adam.

Jesus says, "When the Advocate comes, whom I will send to you from the Father, the Spirit of truth who comes from the Father, this Paraclete will testify on my behalf. You also are to testify" (Jn 15:26–27).

What is the testimony of the Spirit? The Spirit will witness to the unconditional love of God that became available to us through Jesus. This divine love, as it becomes manifest within the structures of the world, is a light in the darkness. It is a light that the darkness cannot accept. The divine love of God reveals to us that fruitfulness is more important than success, that the love of God is more important than the praise of people, that community is more important than individualism, and compassion more important than competition. In short, the light of the Spirit reveals to us that love conquers all fear. But the world rules by fear. Without fear the world doesn't know how to control or govern.

The Spirit's testimony threatens the world. It is not surprising that anyone who testifies with the Spirit is a danger to the world. That is why Jesus predicts, "An hour is coming when those who kill you will think that by doing so they are offering worship to God. And they will do this because they have not known the Father or me" (Jn 16:2–3).

These words are very relevant in our days. When we do not live in deep communion with God — that is, with the Spirit of Jesus within us — then religion is easily put into the service of our desire for success, fame, and stardom. From that place we are willing to "kill" whoever is in the way of reaching our goal. The tragedy is that indeed we quickly convince ourselves that we do the killing in God's name. This is how many Indians, Jews, and Muslims have lost their lives. This is part of what gives a religious rationalization for violence in Northern Ireland, Bosnia, and many other places.

Jesus wants us not to be surprised when these things happen. He says, "I have said these things to you so that when their hour comes you may remember that I told you about them" (Jn 16:4).

We talked about these things during the Eucharist this morning and became aware of how often we, as church, have hurt each other in the Name of God. Many of the people around the table had had painful experiences in their church, or with their parents and friends. They were surprised when family members and religious people wounded them so deeply. Sometimes, because of the pain, they had left the church, but by doing so they lost contact with the message of Jesus.

The words of Jesus are very important. They warn us that this will happen, and they prepare us for this very experience of pain. Jesus' prediction may help us not to reject the love of God even when we are rejected in God's Name.

Tuesday, May 14

Jesus says, "If you keep my commandments, you will abide in my love, just as I have kept my Father's commandments and abide in God's love" (Jn 15:10). Jesus invites me to abide in his love. That means to dwell with all that I am in him. It is an invitation to a total belonging, to full intimacy, to an unlimited being-with.

The anxiety that has plagued me during the last week shows that a great part of me is not yet "abiding" in Jesus. My mind and heart keep running away from my true dwelling place, and they explore strange lands where I end up in anger, resentment, lust, fear, and anguish. I know that living a spiritual life means bringing every part of myself home to where it belongs.

Jesus describes the intimacy that he offers as the connectedness between the vine and its branches. I long to be grafted onto Jesus as a branch onto the vine so that all my life comes from the vine. In communion with Jesus, the vine, my little life can grow and bear fruit. I know it, but I do not live it. Somehow I keep living as if there are other sources of life that I must explore, outside of Jesus. But Jesus keeps saying, "Come back to me, give me all your burdens, all your worries, fears, and anxieties. Trust that with me you will find rest." I am struggling to listen to that voice of love and to trust in its healing power.

I deeply know that I have a home in Jesus, just as Jesus has a home in God. I know, too, that when I abide in Jesus I abide with him in God. "Those who love me," Jesus says, "will be loved by my Father" (Jn 14:21). My true spiritual work is to let myself be loved, fully and completely, and to trust that in that love I will come to the fulfillment of my vocation. I keep trying to bring my wandering, restless, anxious self home, so that I can rest there in the embrace of love.

This afternoon Ginny took me to the mall at Short Hills. I found two different sizes of unlined blank books, which I would like to fill with my Adam story. Now I feel new motivation. The new books help!

Wednesday, May 15

. . . I look with some apprehension toward September, because I feel far from ready to end my sabbatical. My mind is fuller than ever with ideas for my writing. I know that my return to Daybreak is only realistic if I continue to do *some* writing, because without it I will dry up interiorly and will quickly feel tired and depressed. I'm grateful that Sue, Nathan, and others at Daybreak agree with me. I am encouraged that they support my desire to build a small house for myself where I will have some space for writing.

If I look back and compare what happened with what I anticipated, I realize that I can't fruitfully predict what will happen. God must remain the God of surprises.

Thursday, May 16

Jesus said to his disciples, "A little while, and you will no longer see me, and again a little while, and you will see me" (Jn 16:16).

Life is "a little while," a short moment of waiting. But life is not empty waiting. It is to wait full of expectation. The knowledge that God will indeed fulfill the promise to renew everything, and will offer us a "new heaven and a new earth," makes the waiting exciting. We can already see the beginning of the fulfillment. Nature speaks of it every spring; people speak of it whenever they smile; the sun, the moon, and the stars speak of it when they offer us light and beauty; and all of history speaks of it when amidst all devastation and chaos, men and women arise who reveal the hope that lives within them.

This "little while" is a precious time. It is a time of purification and sanctification, a time to be prepared for the great passage to the permanent house of God. What is my main task during my "little while"? I want to point to the signs of the Kingdom to come, to speak about the first rays of the day of God, to witness to the many manifestations of the Holy Spirit among us. I do not want to complain about this passing world but to focus on the eternal that lights up in the midst of the temporal. I yearn to create space where it can be seen and celebrated.

Every day at the communion table I experience unity and peace growing among us. This is a glimpse of the Kingdom during my "little while."

Friday, May 17

Much of today was getting ready for my trip to Santa Fe. Tomorrow I will fly to Albuquerque and drive from there to Santa Fe to spend a week writing under the supervision and mentorship of Jim. I am very much looking forward to seeing Jim again and discussing with him not only the subject but also the craft of my writing.

Sunday, May 19

Today I had a memorable lunch with Jim. Although I had come to Santa Fe to ask for Jim's help in my writing, our first conversation has focused on what to do with our lives between ages sixty and eighty.

For me this is an increasingly important question, which is not without anxiety. Over the years I have built up a certain reputation. People think of me as a Catholic priest, a spiritual writer, a member of a community with mentally handicapped people, a lover of God, and a lover of people. It is wonderful to have such a reputation. But lately I find I get caught in it and I experience it as restricting. Without wanting to, I feel a certain pressure within me to keep living up to that reputation and to do, say, and write things that fit the expectations of the Catholic Church, L'Arche, my family, my friends, my readers. I'm caught because I'm feeling that there is some kind of an agenda that I must follow in order to be faithful.

But since I am in my sixties, new thoughts, feelings, emotions, and passions have arisen within me that are not all in line with my previous thoughts, feelings, emotions, and passions. So I find myself asking, "What is my responsibility to the world around me, and what is my responsibility to myself? What does it mean to be faithful to my vocation? Does it require that I be consistent with my earlier way of living or thinking, or does it ask for the courage to move in new directions, even when doing so may be disappointing for some people?"

I am more and more aware that Jesus died when he was in his early thirties. I have already lived more than thirty years longer than Jesus. How would Jesus have lived and thought if he had lived that long? I don't know. But for me many new questions and concerns emerge at my present age that weren't there in the past. They refer to all the levels of life: community, prayer, friendship, intimacy, work, church, God, life, and death. How can I be free enough and let the questions emerge without fearing the consequences? I know I am not yet completely free because the fear is still there.

Jim is sixty-two years old. I am sixty-four. We both are asking the question about how we live between sixty and eighty. The difference is that Jim is bound neither by his reputation nor by any institution, so he is very free, and he loves his freedom. It's quite an experience for me to meet such a man.

Jim seems genuinely interested in my life and writing too, without having any other goal in mind except to help me to claim what is mine. He seems to have no agenda. He doesn't seem to want me to conform to any of his ideas. I trust that God put this man in my path for a good reason.

Tuesday, May 21

During and after lunch Jim and I talked about the Adam book. Jim was clear that poverty was the most important concept of the book. He said, "Poverty is being empty of adverse human influences. When you are completely free from these influences, you are open to the Divine. In his poverty Adam appears to have been fully open to the Divine, and thus he helped you to become more aware of the Divine within yourself." Jim's Christian Science background made him identify with what I was trying to say about Adam.

Jim feels that Adam's life gives expression to the presence of the Divine in our lives, but he is convinced that the book is not only about Adam but also about me and about my own spiritual search. He encouraged me to share about the ways that Adam touched and shaped my life.

I become aware of how my own needs for friendship, human contact, and intimacy are still part of "worldly" influences. Adam, who appeared so deeply disabled, had a divine gift for me. Others who appear gifted, or who offer me something other than the Divine, leave me, finally, with empty hands. Sharing his experiences of human relationships, Jim concluded by saying, "There are no shortcuts to the Divine. Success, sex, power, and fame will not give us what we need. On the contrary, we often have to lose them all in order to discover the truth of the good, present, and active God within us. Your relationship with Adam has taught you a lot about this."

Wednesday, May 22

Today I spent the day with a friend. When I got back to Malcolm's condominium at 7:00 p.m., I discovered that I had lost my house key. I panicked because I had locked the front door and the gate of the house. Frantically I kept going through all my pockets, but no key. Finally I drove to a public phone and tried to call Malcolm in Fort Worth to ask him what to do, but he wasn't home. Then I called Jim, who was busy with a client on another line. I said, "I am home, but can't get in. I have no idea what to do, but I will retrace my steps. Maybe I dropped the key." Jim said, "Keep calm, stay there, and call me back in a few minutes so we can figure something out."

Meanwhile, the sun was going down. I wondered to myself if perhaps the key had fallen in the condominium parking lot, so I decided to go and look while I was waiting. Just before I arrived at the place, I said to St. Anthony, "Please help me find the keys. Please. I promise that I will give a nice gift to someone who needs it." I was surprised by my own prayer. I had not prayed like that since I was a child, and I cannot remember ever praying to St. Anthony before tonight.

It was getting quite dark as I stepped out of my car and let my eyes go over the parking place. I didn't see anything at first, so I kept looking. And suddenly, there was something red on the asphalt. I bent over and picked up my key! I cried out, "Thank you, St. Anthony, thank you, thank you." I called Jim and said, "Please come over to celebrate my key!" He came, and we laughed a lot. I wondered, "To whom shall I give St. Anthony's reward?"

Peapack, Saturday, May 25

The last day of the Easter season. I am deeply moved by the final scene in the Gospel of John. After Jesus has called Peter to follow him, Peter points to the "beloved disciple," and says, "Lord, what about him?" Jesus answers, "If it is my will that he remain until I come, what is that to you? Follow me!" (Jn 21:21–22). How often do I say, "What about him, her, them, this, or that?" I keep raising questions that seem to be expressions of concern but are in fact signs of my lack of trust. There are so many "yes, but" remarks in my life. "Yes, I will follow you, but tell me first what is going to happen with my family, my friends, my career, my future plans." Jesus answers, "Don't worry about all of that. Trust me, follow me, and all will be well." It is not surprising that my life is so fragmented. Many worries keep pulling me away from the center, thus dividing my life. I want to believe in my call to follow Jesus and to trust that everything else will fall into place because I do believe that He holds the whole world safely in the palms of his hands.

◆ ◆ ◆

This afternoon my sister, Laurien, and her companion, Henri, arrived. The sun was shining brightly and the valley more beautiful than ever. We took a little walk along the river and then had dinner with Peggy.

Pentecost Sunday, May 26

In the letter to the Galatians Paul writes, "The fruits of the Spirit are love, joy, peace, patience, kindness, goodness, trustfulness, gentleness and self-control; no law can touch such things as these" (Gal 5:22–23). During the Pentecost celebration we talked about these fruits and their meaning in our lives. Peggy made a large plate with nine fruits, each "named" for one of the spiritual fruits, and seven-year-old Rush went around the circle inviting each person to take the one fruit that they would most like grow within them.

It was a joyful event. Beautiful flowers, brought by Joanie; altar bread made by Carol and Peggy; readings read by Clair and Jane; plus songs and prayers. It was a very intimate celebration of the Eucharist with about twenty people.

Memorial Day, Monday, May 27

Close to thirty people came to the morning Eucharist! It was clear that this Monday holiday permitted people to come with their families to participate in the morning's celebration.

The Gospel about the rich young man who loved Jesus and was loved by him but couldn't follow him because of his attachment to his many possessions was a real challenge for us. What seemed to impress people was the realization that this story does not imply a huge leap from everything to nothing but rather a long series of small steps in the direction of love. The tragedy for the rich young man was not that he was unwilling to give up his wealth — who would be? The real tragedy for him was that he missed something both he and Jesus desired, which was the opportunity to develop a deep and intimate relationship. It is not so much a question of detachment as it is a question of fully trusting and following the voice of love. Detachment is only a consequence of a greater attachment. Who would worry about his few possessions when invited to be intimate with the Lord of abundance, who offers more fish than we can catch and more bread than we can eat? What would have happened if the young man had said yes to Jesus? Wouldn't he, just like the other disciples, have become a source of hope for countless people? Now he drops out of history and is never heard of again! What a loss! To follow the voice of love, step by step, trusting that God will give us all we need is the great challenge.

New York, Tuesday, May 28

This afternoon I arrived at 5:00 p.m. at the Crossroad offices. Gwendolin, Bob, and I talked for a few minutes about the text of the first eight months of my sabbatical journal, which I had sent them a few weeks ago. They both responded warmly to what I had written, gave me some notes they had made about the parts that spoke most to them, and wondered how I could most effectively integrate the best stories with the best meditations. I realize that I still have three months of my sabbatical left and will write a lot more before this journal is finished, but it is good to gradually discover which of all these pages are worth presenting to a large readership.

Peapack, Wednesday, May 29

I stayed in New York with Wendy and Jay, and after a very quiet Eucharist in their living room this morning, I took a cab to Port Authority and a bus back to Peapack. It was a nice day in New York, but I am glad to be back in this quiet place.

Friday, May 31

Today is the Feast of the Visitation. A very young girl meets a very old woman. Both are pregnant. Both feel misunderstood. Joseph, the young girl's fiancé, is considering separation, fearing scandal. Zechariah, the old woman's husband, has been struck dumb and doesn't understand what's happening. And the women themselves, do they know? Hardly. They are puzzled, confused, and somewhat lost.

Mary, the young girl, needs to get out of the little gossiping town where she lives. She suffers from staring eyes and whispers behind her back. She escapes. In haste she goes over the hills to Ain Karim, where her old cousin Elizabeth lives. She knows deep within her that Elizabeth will understand and offer her a safe place to wait for the child.

As they meet and look at each other, they shout with joy. They embrace, they hold each other, they cry, they laugh. The fear and self-consciousness fall away from both of them.

"The mother of my Lord," cries Elizabeth. "My soul magnifies the Lord," cries Mary. Elizabeth understands, affirms, and celebrates. Her whole body is jubilant. The child in her womb leaps with joy. And Mary realizes her grace, her gift, her special blessing. With a newfound freedom she exclaims, "The Lord has looked with favor on the lowliness of this servant. Surely, from now on all generations will call me blessed, for the Mighty One has done great things for me" (Lk 1:43, 46–49).

Two women who felt oppressed and isolated suddenly realize their greatness and are free to celebrate their blessing. The two of them become community. They need each other, just to be together and protect each other, support each other, and affirm each other. They stay together for three months. Then each of them is ready to face her truth alone, without fear, willing to suffer the consequences of her motherhood.

I can hardly think about a better way to understand friendship, care, and love than "the way of the visitation." In a world so full of shame and guilt, we need to visit each other and offer each other a safe place where we can claim our freedom and celebrate our gifts. We need to get away once in a while from the suspicious voices and angry looks and be in a place where we are deeply understood and loved. Then we might be able to face the hostile world again, without fear and with new trust in our integrity.

June 1996

Monday, June 3

Lorenzo is a Roman nobleman. Presently he is an assistant woodworker in the Daybreak woodery. Lorenzo is a simple man with deep convictions, a strong prayer life, and a great desire to serve the poor. He is gentle, kind, faithful, and upright in everything he says and does.

The story of his youth in a palazzo in Rome, of his studies in the United States, and of his life with people with mental disabilities in Canada is basically very unsensational. It is the story of a wounded heart in search of a vocation. It is the story of a soul. But in all its simplicity and straightforwardness, it is a story full of light. Francesco, Lorenzo's brother, made an audiotape on which he describes Lorenzo as a man of stability and determination, and as one having clear goals in the midst of a world full of social busyness, partygoing, unfocused living, and spiritual flatness.

Whenever Lorenzo goes home he feels the difference between the lifestyle of his family and his life in the Daybreak community. Sometimes he feels seduced by the many voices questioning why he is wasting his life with such unsophisticated people when in Italy he could enjoy more comforts and pleasures. But when he returns after a visit to Italy he feels at home, surrounded by his people at Daybreak.

I think it is good to write down Lorenzo's story. It is a story of simple sanctity in the midst of an ambitious and competitive world.

Wednesday, June 5

Lorenzo had written a few notes about simplicity to help me in my writing about his life. He feels that simplicity is one of his main characteristics. He wrote, "Simplicity is finding pleasure and enjoyment in the small and ordinary things of life. Simplicity is the total surrender to that inner core where the spirit of each being exists. It enables us to experience being part of creation and its beauty."

What Lorenzo had to say about simplicity clearly comes from his heart. I wonder if *simplicity* is not the core word around which I should write his biography.

At 10:30 a.m. Steve arrived. Steve is a friend and artist from Newburyport, Massachusetts. He made the cover for the book *With Burning Hearts* and has agreed to make cover images for the hardback volumes of my "collected works" that Continuum will publish. The idea is to make a series of drawings of hands: blessing hands, healing hands, speaking hands, giving hands, and so on. Steve wanted to use my own hands for these drawings. So he came to take photographs of my hands.

It was a beautiful day with magnificent light. Steve took hundreds of pictures in the garden. While he was taking these pictures, I became aware of how many things hands can express: joy, anger, love, care, gentleness, support, and more.

After lunch Lorenzo got "into the act," and we made many photographs of our four hands, holding, touching, pulling, pushing, grasping, slapping, et cetera. We also used a cup with wine and a plate with bread, to express giving and receiving.

Thursday, June 6

"You shall love the Lord your God with all your heart, and with all your soul, and with all your mind, and with all your strength. You shall love your neighbor as yourself" (Mk 12:29–31). This morning during the Eucharist we reflected on these words. The love of God, neighbor, and self is one love. This great commandment is a call to the most profound unity, in which God, God's people, and we ourselves are part of one love. In this way the great commandment is much more than a moral prescription. It is a mandate to always, in all things, and at all places live and work for oneness. All that exists is one. It is all part of the all-embracing divine love. Our call is to make that love visible in our daily lives.

This unity can be seen in three ways. First, when we direct our whole beings toward God, we will find our neighbor and ourselves right in the heart of God. Second, when we truly love ourselves as God's beloved children, we will find

185

ourselves in complete unity with our neighbor and with God. Third, when we truly love our neighbor as our brother and sister, we will find, right there, God and ourselves in complete unity. There really is no first, second, and third in the great commandment. All is one: the heart of God, the hearts of all people, our own hearts. All the great mystics have "seen" this and lived it.

Friday, June 7

The Eucharist was very special today because of the presence of Amy, a lovely wife and mother of two children who is suffering from advanced brain cancer. Her friend, a medical doctor, brought her in a wheelchair. She was laid on the large sofa right in front of the altar table. Around her was a circle of about twenty people.

After the reading of the Beatitudes I spoke about us as a community of the weak held together by mutual forgiveness and celebration. At the conclusion of the Eucharist we all blessed Amy, asking God for healing in her body, mind, and heart. Amy herself was very open and shared her immense frustration that God had not heard her prayers and performed a miracle. At this moment she was clearly not yet in a spiritual place where she could prepare herself for her death. But she was deeply grateful for the prayers of our little community.

Tomorrow will be a very busy day. I'll be driving Lorenzo to the airport, driving to Princeton for the wedding of Bobby and Anne, bringing the car back to Peapack, packing for the trip to Holland, and going by bus to New York to stay with Wendy and Jay. I hope all goes well, but I get nervous just thinking about it.

Geysteren, Sunday, June 16

After many embraces, kisses, and handshakes, Franz, Reny, and I were on our way to Geysteren [near the beginning of Nouwen's five-week trip to Europe]. Shortly after 3:00 p.m. we arrived at my father's home. He was very glad to have Franz and Reny as his guests, especially since they both had been so kind and generous to us during our trip to Freiburg at Christmastime.

At 6:00 p.m. my brother Paul, my brother Laurent and his wife, Heiltjen, and my sister, Laurien, with her partner, Henri, arrived, and all of us went out for dinner at my father's favorite restaurant. . . .

Rotterdam, Wednesday, June 19

This afternoon I took the train to Rotterdam, where I was invited to animate the conversation of a theological club of Catholics that has been meeting monthly for the last twenty years. I felt a real spiritual interest. Good questions emerged such as, How should I pray? How can I keep focused on God? How can we live spiritual lives when we have very competitive jobs? What disciplines can be of help? People were kind, direct, open, loving, and very attentive. I was deeply moved by their interest in L'Arche. At the end of the evening, I had a sense of having met a unique group of Dutchmen, whom I would love to come to know more personally.

Geysteren, Thursday, June 20

Early in the morning I took the train to Utrecht, where I had been invited to speak at the biweekly meeting of the deans of the archdiocese....

After the deans' meeting I took the train to Venray and a cab to my father's home. Tomorrow my father and I start our vacation together.

Herbeumont, Belgium, Friday, June 21

After our successful trip to Germany over Christmas and New Year's, my father had asked me to accompany him on a ten-day summer vacation to Herbeumont. He had heard that there is a good, quiet hotel here, from which we will be able to make little day trips. I was happy to have another vacation with my father.

Sunday, June 30

The big event tonight was the soccer match between Germany and the Czech Republic. My father and I had an early dinner so we could watch it on TV.

June 1996

I will always remember the Czech goalkeeper. He played an astonishingly good game; many times he prevented the Germans from scoring. His agility, courage, foresight, and iron nerves made him in my eyes the great hero. But in overtime, when the match was 1–1, he couldn't hold on to the ball that the German player shot into his hands, so he was the reason why the Germans, not the Czechs, received the European Cup from Queen Elizabeth. He will be remembered not as a hero but as the man who failed to give the Czech Republic its victory. While the Germans were dancing on the field, embracing one another, crying with joy, and raising their arms victoriously, this talented goalkeeper sat against one of the goalposts, his head buried in his knees. Nobody was there with him. He was the loser.

I feel deeply moved by the image of the defeated goalkeeper. All his great performances will be forgotten, in light of the one mistake that cost the Czechs the greatly desired European Cup. I often wonder about this "final mistake." After a long and fruitful life, one unhappy event, one mistake, one sin, one failure can be enough to create a lasting memory of defeat. For what will we be remembered? For our many acts of kindness, generosity, courage, and love, or for the one mistake we made toward the end? "Yes, he was fabulous, but he failed." "Yes, she was a saintly person, but she sinned." "Yes, they were great, but at the end they disappointed us."

Sometimes I think about dying before the great mistake! What if the "saints" had lived longer and had not been able to keep the ball in their hands at the final moment? Would such a small mistake have brought their saintliness to nothing? It frightens me to think this way. I realize that finally human beings are very fickle in their judgments. God and only God knows us in our essence, loves us well, forgives us fully, and remembers us for who we truly are.

July 1996

Geysteren, Tuesday, July 2

It has been so good to have another pleasant and peaceful vacation with my father. Although he was suffering physically, he was interested in dialoguing about many things that interest him and interest me. Our trip today was pleasant and uneventful, and we got home about 3:00 p.m.

After supper my father went to bed and I watched a most interesting documentary about the life and work of Igor Sikorsky, the inventor and producer of the helicopter. His story is the story of a Russian boy obsessed with the idea of building a plane that could fly vertically as well as horizontally. Against all odds he kept working on his project. After the Bolshevik Revolution in 1917, seeing that many czarist pilots were being executed, Sikorsky fled Russia and eventually made it to the United States. There, with incredible tenacity and will power, he developed the helicopter and built one of the largest helicopter industries in the world.

More than anything it was the determined character of Igor Sikorsky that fascinated me. If I could be half as determined in realizing my vocation as Igor was in realizing his dream —

as a young boy he actually had a dream in which he saw his helicopter — I would be able to help a lot of people to fly!

Oberursel, Germany, Monday, July 8

At 2:00 p.m. I had a fast and easy train ride to Oberursel, where Rodleigh was waiting. This Monday is one of the few days during the season that the circus has no show. It was good to see the Flying Rodleighs again. They were in good spirits and happy with the new shape of their trapeze act. Since I last saw them, Rodleigh and Karlene's oldest brother, Quentin, had suddenly died at age fifty. That was very painful. But Rodleigh and Jennie also had good news to share; they are expecting a baby in December.

Last year Jennie had stopped flying because of increasing shoulder pains but also because of her hope of having a baby before getting too old. Except for the bad weather the season has been good so far. A good show, a good trapeze act, and often a full tent.

Still, from all the stories it became clear that the Flying Rodleighs are gradually coming to the end of their years as a trapeze troupe. They had signed a contract for the 1997 March–November season, but that may be their final year. Rodleigh, Karlene, and Jonathon are beginning to feel more fatigue, more stress, more pains. Last year Jonathon had knee surgery. "I am fine now," he said, "but I got a warning. It might be time to start thinking about something else."

It has been more than five years since I met the Rodleighs in Freiburg. At that time they had just started to work for this circus. They hadn't expected to stay this long because the circus director seldom hires an act for more than three seasons. Next year will be their eighth with this circus.

I never expected to become so close to this wonderful group of people. Every time I meet them again I feel excited and grateful. The book I want to write about them still has not been written, but I trust that it will be. Maybe our long friendship will allow me to write something quite different from an interesting story about the trapeze. The spectacular trapeze act has gradually moved out of the center of my attention and become little more than the background of the lives of eight people who struggle to work and love well in our contemporary society.

Jonathon and Karlene offered me hospitality in their caravan. I can sleep on their "living room sofa." I am very tired and happy to lay down after a long day.

Tuesday, July 9

After a long sleep and a relaxed breakfast with Jonathon and Karlene, I wrote for an hour in this journal and then walked with Jonathon to the tent where Rodleigh, John, Slava, and Jonathon were going to level the rigging. They had set it all up yesterday but still needed to do the fine tuning of the cables, poles, swings, and so on. Every new place requires a careful checking of distances, floor level, heights, and many other details. A trapeze act is such precision work that small irregularities in the rigging can be fatal.

I am suddenly aware of how intimate the circus tent is. Last year and the year before last I saw the Rodleighs performing in halls in Rotterdam and Zwolle that could seat sixty thousand people or more. There the trapeze act took place at a great distance and lost some of its warmth. Now I can see it in its normal surroundings.

The 3:30 p.m. show brought in hundreds of children. I hadn't expected that I would be so moved seeing the Rodleighs again, but I found myself crying as I watched them flying and catching under the big top. Their act was a lot better than when I saw them last year at the winter circus. The choreography was elegant; there were many wonderful surprises, and the whole performance felt very energetic. Even though I have seen the Flying Rodleighs for five years now and have attended dozens of their shows, they never bore me. There always seems to be something new, something original, something fresh. I can understand why they are continually offered new contracts.

As I watched them in the air, I felt some of the same profound emotion as when I saw them for the first time with my father in 1991. It is hard to describe, but it is the emotion coming from the experience of an enfleshed spirituality. Body and spirit are fully united. The body in its beauty and elegance expresses the spirit of love, friendship, family, and community, and the spirit never leaves the here and now of the body.

Wednesday, July 10

This morning I visited Jennie in her trailer just to ask her about the baby. She is so beautiful as an expectant mother. We had quite a discussion and even spoke about what would happen if the baby had Down's syndrome or any other abnormalities. Jennie's main concern was that Rodleigh might have to leave the circus if there were problems with the baby. Hopefully these decisions won't be necessary.

At noon I went to the tent to see the practice session. Rodleigh was teaching Slava the triple somersault. He makes the triple into the net all right, but so far he has not been able to reach catchpoint with John. They have been touching hands, but that is all.

At the end of the practice session, Rodleigh asked me if I would like to make a swing or two. I said, "Sure, I'd love to." First he helped me get into the net and showed me how to climb the long ladder to the pedestal. It is an intimidating place to be. The space below, above, and around me felt enormous and awesome. Kerri and Slava pulled me up onto the pedestal, put the safety belt around me, held me tight, and handed me the bar. As I held the bar I wondered if I would be able to hold my own weight, but when they pushed me off I felt at ease swinging above the net a few times. I tried to kick

195

a little to get higher but simply didn't have much breath left, so Rodleigh told me how to drop into the net. I repeated the whole sequence once more with a tiny bit more grace. Then Rodleigh agreed to give me a sense of the catcher's grip. So I climbed the ladder on the catcher's side, and Jonathon, who was hanging head down on the catchbar, grabbed me by my wrists and held me hanging there for a while. I looked up into his upside-down face and could imagine how it would be to swing while being held by him. Altogether I was happy with the experience. It got me as close as I will ever come to being a trapeze artist! . . .

Sunday, July 14

. . . It is clear that those who practice Christianity in this city are a tiny minority of the people. Near the cathedral a skinhead walked up to me and said, "I went into that church and gave them a guilder! You think they would let me stay in there with my head shaved like this?" I said, "Sure, you are very welcome to go there, and you don't have to give any more money!" I wonder if he did. The distance between this boy and the ceremonies in the cathedral seems huge, but is it really? Since the CD with Gregorian music became so popular among the rock youth, I am less sure about it all. Maybe many skinheads are waiting to be welcomed!

Peapack, Tuesday, July 16

At 2:00 p.m. Wendy took me to Port Authority, and at 4:20 p.m. I arrived at Bernardsville, where Ginny was waiting for me. I was exhausted but too curious about what was in the mail to go to bed.

-Thursday, July 18

There were many new people at the Eucharist this morning. We talked about connecting our burdens with the burden of Jesus, which is a "light" burden even though it is the burden of all humanity. A burden, even a small one, when carried alone and in isolation can destroy us, but a burden when carried as part of God's burden can lead us to new life. This is the great mystery of our faith.

◆ ◆ ◆

I had a lot of telephone conversations with Nathan, Carl, and the architect, Joe, because it looks as if the plans to build my own little apartment can be realized in the fall. They want me to come to Toronto on Friday to finalize the plans.

Thursday, July 25

During the celebration of this morning's Eucharist in honor of St. James, I spoke about Jesus' question to James and John, "Can you drink the cup?" and summarized the book I wrote about the question. Blair, who raises challenging questions, asked, "But what if I really do not want to drink my cup?" I responded by speaking a little about the tension between wanting and not wanting, being able and not being able, and about how that tension can best be lived in a loving community.

In the evening Peggy took me to the house of friends for dinner where several others had been invited and where we had a good discussion about politics and religion. A Democratic senator was pondering how to influence people the most — as a politician who is able to introduce laws that can help millions of people, or as a minister who continues to offer hope and consolation to people in their daily struggle? These seemed to be life issues for the people present.

For me it is not a question of how we can most influence others. What matters is our vocation. To what or whom are we called? When we make the effect of our work the criterion of our sense of self, we end up very vulnerable. Both the political and the ministerial life can be responses to a call. Both too can be ways to acquire power. The final issue is not the result of our work but the obedience to God's will, as long as we realize that God's will is the expression of God's love.

Monday, July 29

Joanie and Jim invited Nathan and me for dinner with Therese and Bill and Judith. Bill is known for his TV programs with Joseph Campbell, Huston Smith, and other American thinkers and writers. Therese is a harpist-singer who founded the Chalice of Repose Project, at a hospital in Montana.

Bill is a professional listener. That became evident tonight. He systematically asked Nathan and me about our lives, our community, our spiritual vision and future plans. When later Therese came, he gave her equal time. Bill was, long ago, ordained as a Baptist minister but has worked his whole life in communications: newspapers and television. He and his wife are deeply spiritual people with a great desire to offer vision to the American culture. In many ways Bill makes me think of Fred, even though his work for TV is very different from Fred's. But, like Fred, Bill is clearly committed to bringing "good news" to TV; he is independent, hardworking, and produces programs that stand out by their relevance, educational value, and spiritual-social vision. Like Fred he is a humble man, truly interested in other people and more concerned with service than with fame....

Tuesday, July 30

It is already two weeks since I returned from Europe, and I still haven't been able to find a good block of time to work on the Adam book. Very frustrating. Everything else seems to take priority: the morning Eucharist, the correspondence, the many calls about layouts and covers of other books, dinners, et cetera. But I want to go back to Adam. It is such an important story. I feel I am saying something fresh and original.

The vision that the story of Jesus allows me to understand Adam while Adam's story makes me understand Jesus keeps fascinating me. Adam is a sacrament, a sacred place where God spoke to me. Remembering Adam is more than thinking about him and praying for him. It is enabling me to keep close to the Jesus I met in and through him. Adam became real to me because Jesus was real to me, and Jesus became real to me became Adam was real to me. Somewhere, somehow, Adam and Jesus are one.

August 1996

Thursday, August 1

Well, Michael Johnson won the gold medal in the 200-meter run as well as in the 400-meter run. A "history-making event." In the 200 meter he also broke the world record. The commentators speak about the fastest man in history. To describe his spirit they said, "He doesn't take prisoners, he goes for the kill." But in an interview he expressed a less violent view, "The crowd was wonderful — I never felt so much support. The people are great!"

Donovan Bailey, the Canadian, ran the 100 meter in 9.84 seconds. Michael Johnson ran the 200 meter in 19.34. The greatest speed ever! And what about the pressure of millions watching you and expecting you to win? Michael said, "I can't even describe the pressure, but that's what makes it all happen!"

The unrelenting emphasis on winning the gold makes it hard to watch these Olympic games. They become an emotional roller coaster. It is hard for me to believe that all the pressure, all the intensity, all the winning and losing contribute to a peaceful and compassionate world. There is little if any "play" left in the games. Competition is the core word, and the tears of the losers as well as of the winners are not tears of a contrite or grateful heart. How possibly can they heal our world? Still ... I, with millions of other people, keep watching and admiring those who go beyond what we thought to be the limit of human possibilities.

Nathan and I had a peaceful day. We both spent a lot of time in our rooms working.

Friday, August 2

When Jesus came to his hometown and began to teach the people in the synagogue, they said: "Isn't this the carpenter's son? Is not his mother called Mary? And are not his brothers James and Joseph and Simon and Judas? And are not all his sisters with us? Where then did this man get all this? And they took offense at him" (Mt 13:54–58). It fascinates me that Jesus finally had to establish his authority outside the circle of his family and friends. All we know about his relationship with his parents is his taking distance from them: in the temple when he was twelve years old, in Cana when Mary wanted to intervene, during his preaching or when the family wanted to visit him.

Family is where we grow up into adult, mature people, but we have to leave our families to fulfill our deepest vocation. Family can give us a sense of belonging, but in order to claim our deepest belonging, our belonging to God, we have to move away from those who pretend to know us and discover the deepest source of our lives. Our parents, brothers, and sisters do not own us. Without leaving them it is hard to fully become free and listen to the One who called us even before we were born.

Jesus often had to say no to his family in order to be able to say a full yes to his Father in heaven.

Saturday, August 3

Today's Gospel reading about the death of John the Baptist made me think about servant leadership. John the Baptist certainly was one of the most important spiritual leaders of his time, but his whole mission was geared to put Jesus into the light. All he did and said finally served to create the space for Jesus' leadership.

Robert Greenleaf and many of his students have developed the concept of servant leadership in ways that it also could be a guiding concept in contemporary business and management. A good leader is able to "decrease" so that others can "increase." It certainly requires a great inner strength and confidence to "let go" of the dominant position and let others develop their leadership with your affirmation and support. It is no secret that in church and society many leaders cling to their positions as long as they can.

Sunday, August 4

During the Eucharist we had a very lively discussion about the Gospel of the multiplication of bread. What we give away multiplies, and what we hoard becomes less. One of the participants was especially intrigued with the thought that the multiplication of bread might in fact have been the result of people's willingness to share the little they had with their neighbors. The true miracle might have been not that Jesus made many loaves out of a few but that he called people to not cling to their own food but trust that there was enough for everyone. If this generosity would be practiced universally in our world, there would not be so many starving people. But this is also the eucharistic vision: Jesus shares his Body and Blood so that we all can become a living Christ in the world. Jesus himself multiplies through giving himself away. We become the body of Christ, individually as well as communally. . . .

Tuesday, August 6

The Feast of the Transfiguration! When and where do we have an experience of God's Glorious Presence, an experience of unity, an experience of inner fulfillment, an experience of light in the darkness? Peter says: "You do well to be attentive to this as to a lamp shining in a dark place, until the day dawns and the morning star rises in your hearts" (2 Pt 1:19).

Maybe we do not always fully recognize our mountaintop experiences; we write them off as insignificant and trivial compared with all the important and urgent things we have to do. Still, Jesus wants us to see his glory, so that we can cling to that experience in moments of doubt, despair, or anguish. When we are attentive to the light within us and around us, we will gradually see more and more of that light and even become a light for others.

We have to trust that the transfiguration experience is closer to us than we might think. Trusting that, we may also be able to live our Gethsemane experience without losing our faith.

Thursday, August 8

My good old friend Dean drove from Middletown, Connecticut, to Peapack to spend the day with me. I have a deep admiration for Dean. He always challenges me. He calls me to a radical faith, a deep commitment to the poor, a prophetic ministry among the rich, and an always closer bond with Jesus. He is my conscience. He loves me but also criticizes me. He cares for me but also unsettles me. He supports me but also calls me to reach out beyond my limits.

Our discussions are always intense, serious, and probing. It is clear to me that this Jewish friend is my prophet. I have to listen to him. If *he* tells me to grow closer to Jesus, I better take that very seriously.

𝒻𝓇𝒾𝒹𝒶𝓎, 𝒜𝓊𝑔𝓊𝓈𝓉 9

"Those who lose their life for my sake will find it," Jesus says. There is no day without many losses. If we are attentive to our inner life, we quickly realize how many times things are not happening in the way we hoped, people aren't saying what we expected, the day is not evolving as we wanted, et cetera, et cetera. All these little "losses" can make us bitter people who complain that life is not fair to us. But if we live these losses for the sake of Jesus — that is, in communion with his redemptive death — then our losses can gradually free us from our self-centeredness and open our hearts to the new life that comes from God. The real question is: "Do I live my losses for my sake or for Jesus' sake?" That choice is a choice for death or life. . . .

𝒮𝒶𝓉𝓊𝓇𝒹𝒶𝓎, 𝒜𝓊𝑔𝓊𝓈𝓉 10

During the Eucharist we spoke about generosity. I was moved by Paul's words: "The one who sows sparingly will also reap sparingly, and the one who sows bountifully will also reap bountifully. Each of you must give as you have made up your mind, not reluctantly or under compulsion, for God loves a cheerful giver. And God is able to provide you with every blessing in abundance, so that by always having enough of everything, you may share abundantly in every good work" (2 Cor 9:6–8).

206

I think that generosity has many levels. We have to think generously, speak generously, and act generously. Thinking well of others and speaking well of others is the basis for generous giving. It means that we relate to others as part of our "gen" or "kin" and treat them as family. Generosity cannot come from guilt or pity. It has to come from hearts that are fearless and free and are willing to share abundantly all that is given to us.

At 5:00 p.m. I drove to Newark Airport to welcome my dear friend Borys. Borys has been teaching summer school at Harvard and is coming to spend some time with me before returning to Ukraine. It was wonderful to see him again. He looked well and was full of enthusiasm. The theological academy in L'viv, of which he is the vice-rector, now has close to six hundred students. Borys said, "It is a once-in-a-millennium opportunity, to affect the future of the Greek Catholic Church." Borys wants to attract the best possible teachers, to collect money to endow chairs, to send Ukrainian students to the West, to build up a theological library, and to find a large building in L'viv to house all his students. . . .

Elmsford, New York,
Monday, August 12

After a very prayerful Eucharist, Borys and I drove to Elmsford, New York. When we arrived we were met by Doug and two Greek Catholic priests. Borys left with the two priests to discuss setting up a foundation in the United States to support the academy in L'viv, and I joined Doug to make an audiotape of *Life of the Beloved*. Borys's visit was a true grace....

Peapack, Tuesday, August 13

... Although I wrote *Life of the Beloved*, I never read it. It is quite an experience to read a book that you yourself wrote more than four years ago. All through I wanted to make changes, rewrite, correct small mistakes, and adapt it to the circumstances of today. But I realized that the best thing would be simply to read it as it was and save my energy for new books. It is amazing how, within a few years, one's ideas and feelings shift. Today I would have written *Life of the Beloved* quite differently. And still, the book continues to be quite popular. That obviously is the reason for making this audiocassette.

Wednesday, August 14

A very busy, somewhat restless day.

During the Eucharist we spoke about dealing with conflict in the community. How to deal with people who sin against us. Jesus is very specific: "If your brother or sister sins against you, go and point out the fault when the two of you are alone." Only when that doesn't help should you call others in, and only when that doesn't help should you "tell it to the church" (Mt 18:15–17). Only when it is clear that the person doesn't want to listen to the church should you leave him or her alone.

It is clear that "confrontation" only is fruitful in love. We have to keep the well-being of the other in mind. But when the other finally does not respond and keeps doing harmful things, then the well-being of the community becomes a priority.

En Route to Cork, Ireland, Monday and Tuesday, August 19 and 20

At 7:40 p.m. my plane left for London. I arrived at 7:30 a.m., and at 10:00 a.m. I was on my way to Cork [for a one-week trip in Ireland].

Cork, Wednesday, August 21

Every time I am in Ireland, I am struck with the different rhythm of life. Because of my jet lag, I decided to "sleep in" until 9:00 a.m. But when I arrived at the breakfast table at 9:30, I was one of the first! No hurry, no urgencies. As they say in Ireland: "God created time, and He created plenty of it."

My visit to Ireland has a long history. In 1961 I presided over the wedding of Sophie and Seamus and in 1966 over the wedding of Leonie and Paddy. Their weddings took place in Holland, but both couples moved to Cork, Ireland, where Seamus is a businessman and Paddy a surgeon.

Last year I came to Ireland to preside over the marriage of David, the oldest child of Sophie and Seamus, to Mary, and now I am here again to celebrate the marriage of Leonietje, the oldest daughter of Leonie and Paddy, to Morgan. Meanwhile Mary and David have their first son, Cian, and I promised to baptize him on Sunday. I wonder if I still will be alive to marry him!

Leonie took me to Oisterhaven, where her family has a summer house overlooking the beautiful bay. When we arrived there I met Leonietje and Morgan for the first time. Wonderful, bright, adventurous people — full of love for their families and, at the same time, quite independent and critical. We had a good long talk about their journeys, their vision of life, and their spiritual attitudes.

After our talk I celebrated the Eucharist for the whole family in the living room. The view is spectacular: a lovely blue bay, green rolling hills surrounding it, a distant view of two rock islands behind which the ocean stretches far and wide, romantic cloud formations letting the bright sun come through here and there, and the trees gently moving in the evening wind. Thanking God in this landscape is easy. Everything speaks of grace and beauty.

We reflected on the story of the workers of the eleventh hour, especially on the words "Are you jealous because I am generous?" (Mt 20:15). When we trust in God's immense love, shouldn't we rejoice when God offers the latecomers as much

210

as those who have worked the whole day? When we experience it as a privilege to work in God's vineyard, why should we be angry that those who came late are treated as equals to those who came long ago? Jealousy is such a divisive emotion. Isn't it possible to truly rejoice when we see someone other than ourselves being given an unexpected gift? The truth, however, is that we can only fully enjoy God's generosity toward others when we truly know how much God loves us.

Much of what we talked about was quite visible in the family that sat around the altar table. I sensed no jealousy, just an immense gratitude that two of them, Leonietje and Morgan, were going to be showered with special love, extra attention, and many, many gifts.

Oisterhaven, Ireland, Thursday, August 22

When I got up this morning, Paddy said, "Well, are you ready for a swim?" It was very cold, but when I got out of the water the warm air created a pleasant sensation and my blood was running fast.

Later in the morning I had another session with Morgan and Leonietje, talking about the details of the marriage ceremony. The rest of the day was full of people, coming in and out with gifts and running left and right to get everything ready for the wedding. I found a quiet corner to read and write a little.

Kenmare, Ireland, Friday, August 23

As Morgan, Leonietje, her sister Rosemary, and I were driving over the small Irish road toward Kenmare, we came across a very serious accident. An American couple with two children had crashed with a young Irish man. Both cars were completely demolished. When we saw the accident we realized that it had just happened. It seemed that the Americans were okay, but the Irish man, David, had hit the front window of his car with his head and was still sitting behind the wheel in a state of shock.

Morgan had a cellular phone and immediately called for an ambulance and for the police. Then both Leonietje and Morgan tried to determine how seriously David was hurt. Morgan made sure that he didn't move to prevent any possible nerve damage, and Leonietje and Morgan both kept talking to him to prevent him from going into deep shock. Meanwhile I talked to the Americans.

What impressed me most was the competent, self-confident, and caring way in which both Morgan and Leonietje responded to the sudden interruption of their journey. They were completely present to the situation and did all the right things. They kept the injured man quiet and still, thus preventing a spinal injury. They also spoke to the police, the American family, the ambulance people, and the local doctor, who came just after the ambulance had arrived. They gave them helpful information, spoke reassuring words, and did everything to prevent confusion or panic.

At 3:00 p.m. we arrived at Kenmare, where the wedding will take place. When evening came all the wedding guests gathered for a barbecue. I was amazed by the people from many parts of the world who had traveled here for this wedding. There was a group of friends from New Zealand and a large group of family from Holland. People had also come from Hong Kong, China, Zimbabwe, South Africa, Denmark, the USA, and England. All together there were about 170 guests, all living together for a weekend.

Talking to so many people from so many parts of the world, I couldn't but marvel at the ways people get connected and grieve for the fact that there still are so many mental, psychological, and religious distances on our small planet. If it is possible to come from the ends of the earth to celebrate the commitment of a man and a woman to each other, why does it remain impossible to stop people from killing each other because of religious, social, and economic differences?

Restless thoughts in the most restful surroundings.

Saturday, August 24

Even though I have been the celebrant at many weddings, every time again I feel quite nervous and anxious. There seem to be so many details that I am seldom very peaceful inside until it is over.

The celebration took place at 2:00 p.m. It was a very beautiful and festive liturgy. The Gospel from John about the great commandment to love one another prompted my words about care: care for your own heart, care for each other, and care for others.

Cork, Sunday, August 25

... After a nice lunch I said good-bye to the bride and groom and as many others as I could, and drove to Cork.

In Cork, David and Mary were waiting for me to baptize Cian, their four-month-old boy. Before the baptism I spoke a little with David and Mary about the significance of baptism. I tried to explain that it is a proclamation that the child is not the property of the parents but a gift of God to be welcomed into the human community and led to the freedom of the children of God. Mary said, "It is often hard to realize that I do not own my little Cian, but as I see him growing so fast I realize that he has been leaving me from the moment he was born. Yes, I feel a certain sadness when I see him growing up so soon."

214

A little later a small circle of family gathered around Cian. He was crying, so we needed time to let him fall asleep and receive all the baptismal blessings. The oils, the water, the white cloth, and the burning candle became real signs of transformation and hope in this small circle of family and friends. David commented that it was "unbelievably special." In such a simple context baptism is not a ritual or a ceremony but an event that directly touches us and affects our lives.

Peapack, Monday, August 26

An endless day! From Cork to London, to Newark, to Peapack. It was a very tiring trip, where I experienced long lines, packed planes, poor food, and bad movies! . . .

Tuesday, August 27

This morning at the Eucharist we spoke about hypocrisy, an attitude that Jesus criticizes. I realize that institutional life leads to hypocrisy, because we who offer spiritual leadership often find ourselves not living what we are preaching or teaching. It is not easy to avoid hypocrisy completely because, wanting to speak in the Name of God, the church, or the larger community, we find ourselves saying things larger than ourselves. I often call people to a life that I am not fully able to live myself.

I am learning that the best cure for hypocrisy is community. When as a spiritual leader I live close to those I care for, and when I can be criticized in a loving way by my own people and be forgiven for my own shortcomings, then I won't be considered a hypocrite.

Hypocrisy is not so much the result of not living what I preach but much more of not confessing my inability to fully live up to my own words. I need to become a priest who asks forgiveness of my people for my mistakes.

◆ ◆ ◆

My sabbatical year is coming to its end. Two more days! Tomorrow Nathan is flying from Toronto to help me move. Thursday morning we will have the last Eucharist in the barn and Thursday night a farewell dinner at Peggy's house. Jay and Wendy will be coming from New York to be part of the farewell from Peapack. Early Friday morning Nathan and I will drive back to Toronto. I am glad, very glad, to be returning to Daybreak, but I also feel that what I have started during this year cannot simply stop. Lots to think about.

Wednesday, August 28

During the Eucharist we spoke about courage. The word *courage* comes from *coeur*, which means "heart." To have courage is to listen to our heart, to speak from our heart, and to act from our heart. Our heart, which is the center of our being, is the seat of courage.

216

Often we debate current issues and express our opinions about them. But courage is taking a stance, even an unpopular stance, not because we think differently from others but because from the center of our being we realize how to respond to the situation we are in. Courage does not require spectacular gestures. Courage often starts in small corners: it is courageous not to participate in gossip, not to talk behind someone's back, not to ridicule another. It is courageous to think well of other people and be grateful to them even when we live different lives than they do. It is courageous to reach out to a poor person, to spend time with a troubled child, to participate in action to prevent war and violence, abuse and manipulation.

Often we praise prophets after they are dead. Are we willing to be prophets while we are alive?

Thursday, August 29

At 9:00 a.m. we celebrated the last Eucharist in the barn — at least for the near future. It was a special celebration with Wendy and Jay from New York, and Nathan from Toronto. After the Gospel some of those present expressed how much this little eucharistic community has come to mean to them during the past six months. Peggy said that it was during the Eucharist in the barn that she had come to the clarity to marry Phil; Ginny spoke about the friendship between us that had developed during these months; Fred expressed how much this community has meant for his priesthood; and quite a few others were simply grateful for the experience.

After the Eucharist there was a wonderful coffee hour with many good cakes to eat, and many warm words of farewell.

The first part of the afternoon was packing. Jay, Wendy, and Ginny all gave a hand to put all my things in boxes and suitcases, and load up my little Honda. The second part I spent with Wendy going through the printed pages of *Bread for the Journey*, which Harper sent us for a final check. Wendy still found many little errors and suggested a few minor changes. I am so grateful to Wendy for doing all this minute work. I wouldn't have the patience or the perseverance to keep reading the same texts again and again and focus on punctuation, correct quotations, capitalization, utilization, and so on. But with Wendy's help we got through the whole manuscript within an hour and a half.

The farewell dinner was at 6:30 p.m. Ginny offered me a beautiful album with photographs of my stay at Peapack. Clair had written very funny titles under the pictures. It was a true work of love. There were even photographs of this morning's liturgy. I was very moved by this beautiful gift and all that Ginny and Clair had done to put it together.

The dinner was delightful and delicious. We all sat outside. It was a nice cool evening and there was much laughter. I thanked everyone for their love and friendship, and expressed how much these months in Peapack had meant to me. Maybe I wrote less than I planned, but I made many new friends, and the development of the eucharistic community had been a unique gift from God. I especially thanked Peggy for being such a beautiful friend. She gave me all the space and freedom I wanted and opened her house and guesthouse to me, my friends, and all the people who came for the daily Eucharist. I also said a special word of thanks to Ginny for all she had done and been for me during the last few months.

It was a beautiful conclusion of my sabbatical year.

Richmond Hill, Friday, August 30

At 7:00 a.m. Nathan and I said good-bye to Peggy and went on our way to Toronto. It was an easy drive. By 6:00 p.m. we were at Daybreak. The last part of the trip — from Buffalo to Toronto — was the hardest because of bumper-to-bumper traffic. It is the beginning of the long weekend, and everyone is on the road.

Kathy, with little Sarah in her arms, and Timmy, welcomed us as we drove in. Also Keith and Jeffi with their little baby, Devon, were there. Timmy was playing basketball, having just gotten a beautiful net for his birthday.

I spent an hour unpacking my things and creating a little order in my little room. And at 8:00 p.m. I went to Kathy's home and had a nice welcome-home meal with Timmy and Sarah.

A little later I was back in my own room again. It was full of flowers — Shiobhan had sent a beautiful basket with lilies, Lorenzo a lovely plant, and Jutta a red bouquet of long-stem carnations and other flowers. There were many balloons and large welcome-home cards with the names and drawings of many community members. What a night! What a warm welcome! Indeed, the sabbatical year is over, and it is good to be back.

Nouwen Book Ideas
for Every Reader

People reading Henri Nouwen for the first time will enjoy *Life of the Beloved: Spiritual Living in a Secular World*. Written as a direct and personal note from Nouwen to a friend with no training in theology or religious thought, this book, with a reflection guide, has become a classic in classrooms and seminaries.

Business, church, and adult education leaders turn to *In the Name of Jesus: Reflections on Christian Leadership* for insight. This book, which helps us understand the special nature of being a leader following Jesus, is widely assigned in seminary and adult education courses and parish training. It includes a study guide.

For daily reflection, turn to *Here and Now: Living in the Spirit*. Use this book for bedside and pocketbook reading, or use it, with the major reflection guide, as the basis for a weekly prayer meeting.

For Lent, keep a copy of *Show Me the Way: Daily Lenten Readings*. Each day includes a scripture verse, reflection, and prayer.

To delve more deeply into Nouwen's thought, especially on the intersection of spirituality and our worldly lives, read Nouwen's challenging *Finding My Way Home: Pathways to Life and the Spirit* (now in paperback, with a reflection guide), and learn about Nouwen's approach to questions of peace, power, and waiting. Then read *Encounters with Merton* to see how the young Henri Nouwen understood the insights of another great spiritual teacher. Finally, *Beyond the Mirror: Reflections on Death and Life* is a short book examining Nouwen's near-death experience and the meaning of life.

True Nouwen fans will appreciate *Sabbatical Journey: The Diary of His Final Year.* This was Nouwen's final book, written in the last year of his life, and is a treasure of intimate details of Nouwen's life and thought. For those new to Nouwen's thought, *Our Second Birth* offers the best of *Sabbatical Journey,* with a focus on Nouwen's reflections about life, suffering, death, and the Christian afterlife.

Crossroad also offers two excellent anthologies of Nouwen's work, prepared by people who knew Nouwen and are committed to preserving his message. Wendy Wilson Greer offers us *The Only Necessary Thing: Living a Prayerful Life,* the finest and most lovingly assembled treasury of Nouwen's work ever prepared. And in *The Heart of Henri Nouwen: His Words of Blessing,* Rebecca Laird and Michael J. Christensen take four key themes Nouwen announces in *Life of the Beloved* and show how they help us understand Nouwen, both as a writer and as a man beloved by those fortunate enough to have known him personally.

For information about Henri Nouwen,
the work of the Henri Nouwen Society,
or to purchase Nouwen books,
please visit *www.HenriNouwen.org.*

To order directly from the publisher,
please call 1-800-707-0670 for Customer Service
or visit our website at *www.cpcbooks.com.*
For catalog orders, please send your request to the address below.

THE CROSSROAD PUBLISHING COMPANY
481 Eighth Avenue, Suite 1550
New York, NY 10001